Backfire Manual
Tactics Against Injustice

Brian Martin

Irene Publishing 2012

First published 2012 by

Irene Publishing, Sparsnäs
irene.publishing@gmail.com

ISBN 978-1-291-14805-3 (paperback)

Most illustrations in this book
are from Wikimedia Commons

Contents

	Author's note	1
1.	The Backfire model	5
2.	Backfire analysis	15
3.	Preparing	43
4.	Now and afterwards	75
5.	Questions and responses	89
6.	Exercises	97
7.	Appendix: Human shields and pre-emptive backfire	103

Author's note

I started studying and promoting nonviolent action in the late 1970s. My special interest was designing society so that nonviolent methods could make militaries unnecessary.

One of the intriguing features of nonviolent action is that when peaceful protesters are brutally attacked, this can lead to greater support for the protesters. The pioneering nonviolence researcher Gene Sharp called this "political jiu-jitsu."[1] In the sport of jiu-jitsu, the opponent's force and momentum can be turned against them. Likewise, protesters, by remaining nonviolent, can turn the attacker's overwhelming force against the attacker, generating greater support.

There are innumerable cases of resistance to injustice. In about 2000, I became interested in situations in which there wasn't much resistance. Two colleagues — Wendy Varney and Adrian Vickers — and I looked at human rights abuses by Indonesian military forces. In some cases, such as the invasion of East Timor, there was plenty of resistance. But in others, there was surprisingly little. In 1965, Indonesian military forces began a massive killing campaign targeted at communists, a campaign considered by many scholars to be genocide. There were perhaps 800,000 victims. There was relatively little resistance within Indonesia and, even more surprisingly, little outrage outside the country. This was a bloodbath welcomed by many anti-communist governments.[2]

---

1 Gene Sharp, *The Politics of Nonviolent Action* (Boston: Porter Sargent, 1973).
2 Brian Martin, Wendy Varney, and Adrian Vickers, "Political Jiu-Jitsu against Indonesian Repression: Studying Lower-profile Nonviolent Resistance," *Pacifica Review*,

I knew about political jiu-jitsu. The victims of the 1965–1966 killings did not resist with any violence. This made me think about why, in some cases, political jiu-jitsu did not happen. I had the idea that the attackers might be doing something to dampen the jiu-jitsu effect. Gradually I developed ideas about methods used by perpetrators to minimise outrage. Because the framework I developed has significant features not included in Sharp's political jiu-jitsu, I called the effect "backfire."

In the past decade I've applied the backfire model to a wide range of cases. It applies readily to massacres of peaceful protesters, for example in East Timor and South Africa. It can also be applied to injustices outside the normal nonviolent-action framework, for example to censorship, sexual harassment, police beatings, torture and genocide.[3]

This manual is designed to provide practical guidance on using the backfire model. It is for those who are taking action against injustice and who want to think carefully about the most effective steps to take.

The backfire model is simply a guide to thinking strategically and tactically. It is not a substitute for thinking. Anyone who is going to be effective needs local knowledge and practical insight. There is no formula for success that will work everywhere on all occasions. The most a model can do is provide reminders about things to take into account.

The most important message from the model is to think about options and to take into account what the other side is likely to do. This is obvious enough when stated this way, but in practice activists often do the things they've always done and think mainly about what they want to achieve and what they plan to do, not what opponents will do.

Chapter 1 introduces the backfire model. Chapter 2 describes backfire analysis: how to discover and understand the tactics

---

[3] For numerous articles, see "Backfire materials," http://www.bmartin.cc/pubs/backfire.html

used by perpetrators of injustice that inhibit outrage. Chapter 3 gives suggestions on preparing for action, taking into account what opponents could do. Chapter 4 gives ideas about taking action while an injustice is occurring, and after the key events are over. Chapter 5 gives responses to some questions about the model.

I have used a few examples, such as police beatings, as examples. You should think of your own examples, preferably issues that you know a lot about, and analyse them. The backfire model is only a set of tools for thinking, not a recipe for action. You need to practise thinking strategically. So think up your own examples. What would you do if a nuclear weapon exploded in a nearby city? What would you do if you discovered a massive government fraud? Chapter 6 has some exercises. You can also develop your own.

There's lots of research on expert performance showing that to become good at something, you need to spend a lot of time practising the most difficult parts of the task.[4] If you want to become good at being an effective activist, you need to spend a lot of time thinking tactically and strategically. The backfire model can be a tool for helping do that.

On my website, I've included lots of articles that use the model. Please send me copies or links so that the information base about the model can be expanded.[5] I'm especially interested in learning about weaknesses in the model and in ways to extend it to new domains, possibly by modifying it. Over the years I've developed and applied the model, it has gradually changed. There's still plenty of room for improvement.

---

4 Readable accounts of research on expert performance include Geoff Colvin, *Talent is Overrated: What Really Separates World-class Performers from Everybody Else* (New York: Penguin, 2010); Daniel Coyle, *The Talent Code. Greatness Isn't Born. It's Grown. Here's How* (New York: Bantam, 2009); David Shenk, *The Genius in All of Us: Why Everything You've Been Told about Genetics, Talent, and IQ Is Wrong* (New York: Doubleday, 2010).

5 Email: bmartin@uow.edu.au

Acknowledgements

I have learned a tremendous amount about backfire from my collaborators and from numerous individuals who have provided comments, references and inspirational practice. Several people offered valuable feedback on drafts of this manual: Sharon Callaghan, Karen Kennedy, Majken Sørensen and Steve Wright. Thanks especially to Jørgen Johansen for his appendix and enthusiastic support.

1. The backfire model

Attacks sometimes backfire. They are counterproductive for the attackers. In fact, they are so disastrous for the attackers that they wish they had never done anything.

- In 1991, Los Angeles police beat a motorist named Rodney King, who had been speeding to avoid arrest. After a video of the beating was broadcast on television, viewers were outraged and public support for the police dropped. The beating backfired on the police.

- In the 1990s, McDonald's sued two anarchists, Helen Steel and Dave Morris, over their leaflet "What's wrong with McDonald's?" The legal action was widely seen as unfair and led to a huge campaign in support of Steel and Morris. It was a public relations disaster for McDonald's. Suing Steel and Morris backfired on McDonald's.

- In 2004, media reported on torture of Iraqi prisoners in Abu Ghraib prison. The graphic photos showed US prison guards grinning as they humiliated and tortured the prisoners. Publication of the photos severely damaged the reputation of the US government, especially in the Middle East. The torture backfired on the US military.

- In 1991, thousands of people joined a funeral procession in Dili, East Timor, using the occasion to peacefully protest against the Indonesian occupation. As the procession entered Santa Cruz cemetery, Indonesian troops suddenly opened fire, killing hundreds of people. Western journalists were present and recorded the massacre. Their testimony and video evidence triggered a huge increase in international support for the East Timorese liberation movement and laid the basis for independence a decade later. The massacre of peaceful protesters backfired on the Indonesian government.

Each of these cases involves an injustice: police brutality, censorship, torture, massacre. In each case those mounting an attack — the police, McDonald's, US prison guards, Indonesian troops — caused damage to their target. But in each case the attack ultimately backfired, causing much greater damage to the attacker and its allies.

Backfires can be immensely valuable in aiding efforts against injustice. The trouble is, most attacks do *not* backfire. Most police beatings receive little or no publicity. Most legal actions for defamation are hardly known. Most torture is done in secret. Even massacres, which are harder to hide, may generate comparatively little concern.

What is going on? Why do some attacks backfire and not others?

The Santa Cruz massacre took place during a 1991 funeral procession to the grave of Sebastião Gomes.

In 1960, there were protests across South Africa against the racist pass laws. In Sharpeville, police opened fire on peaceful protesters, killing perhaps a hundred people. The police and government tried to reduce outrage, but even so the massacre severely damaged the South African government's international reputation.

The backfire model is a way of analysing attacks. It highlights actions taken by each side to reduce or increase outrage from a perceived injustice.

The model is not intended to tell people what to do. Activists know a lot about the local situation and are in the best position to make a judgement about options. The model is a general tool that points to the sorts of things that are likely to happen or that could happen. It can help activists to choose more wisely.

The backfire model, like any model, is a tool. It doesn't guarantee success. Imagine an army that has the best possible strategy. That's helpful, but if the army has few troops, is poorly trained and has outdated weapons, it's unlikely to succeed even with a brilliant strategy. Likewise, the backfire model can help activists develop better strategies, but this isn't a guarantee for success. It is simply one element in a much wider process.

Backfire: the basics

When a powerful group does something unjust, it can take action to reduce popular outrage.

- Cover up the action.
- Devalue the target.
- Reinterpret what happened by lying, minimising, blaming and framing.
- Use official channels to give an appearance of justice.
- Intimidate or reward people involved.

Torture is universally condemned, so when governments use torture, they are likely to use one or more of these techniques to reduce outrage.

Cover up the action

Governments usually carry out torture in secret. Sometimes torturers use methods, such as beating on the soles of the feet, that leave little evidence.

When actions are hidden, outsiders don't even know about them and therefore can't become concerned.

Abu Ghraib prisoner torture.

Devalue the target

Governments claim that prisoners, who are subject to interrogation, are terrorists, criminals, subversives or other undesirable types. When those who are tortured are perceived as dangerous, contemptible or otherwise low in status, then what is done to them may not seem so bad.

Reinterpret what happened by lying, minimising, blaming and framing

When outsiders claim torture is occurring, governments say it isn't: they lie. They say prisoners are being treated well.

When certain methods — such as preventing sleep, waterboarding or sensory deprivation — are known to have been used, governments say they aren't really so bad: no one was seriously hurt. The consequences are said not to be so harmful: they are minimised. Torture methods are labelled abuse or humiliation or something minor — anything but the word torture. Language is used to minimise the seriousness of torture.

Sometimes, governments blame torture on rogue guards acting without authorisation: the guards are blamed so higher officials can avoid responsibility.

Governments say they are using legitimate interrogation techniques to extract information for urgent purposes. This is their point of view. It is a framework or way of looking at the world. Presenting things from a viewpoint is called framing.

Use official channels to give an appearance of justice

Occasionally, claims about torture become so insistent that governments set up an official inquiry, or perhaps prosecute some of those involved. Inquiries and courts usually focus on low-level functionaries, not policy makers, and may apply only light penalties. It might look like justice is being done, but it is a token effort.

Official channels include ombudsmen, courts, commissions of inquiry, panels of experts, grievance procedures and any other formal process for dealing with problems. Official channels usually have the effect of reducing public outrage because people think the problems are actually being dealt with. Official channels are slow, so people's outrage dies down as time passes. Official channels use complex procedures and rely on experts, such as lawyers, so outsiders have little ability to participate or interest in doing so.

Intimidate or reward people involved

Torture is itself a form of intimidation. People who are tortured may be afraid to speak out because of the risk of further torture. In countries with repressive governments, it can be dangerous for others — family members, friends, journalists, human rights groups — to protest against torture, because they might become targets. On the other hand, officials who do the government's bidding may receive rewards, such as pay or promotions.

Intimidation discourages the expression of outrage. People are afraid of the consequences. The possibility of rewards is a temptation to keep quiet or to participate in the actions.

Five methods of reducing outrage and how they relate to an event, perceptions of it, and reactions to it

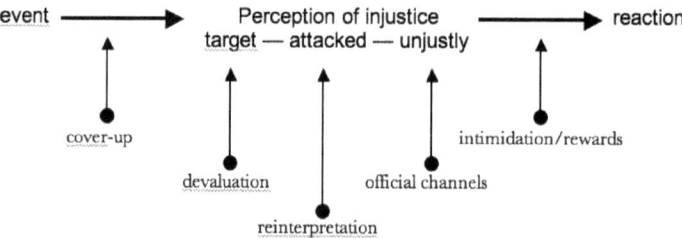

What can be done in the face of these five methods that reduce outrage from injustice? The answer: counter each one of them. Here are the ways.

- Expose what happened.
- Validate the target: show the positive aspects of whoever or whatever is attacked.
- Interpret the events as unjust.
- Mobilise support. Avoid or discredit official channels.
- Resist intimidation and rewards.

Expose what happened.

Opponents of torture can document it and reveal information to the world. This is a primary tool by Amnesty International. Exposure challenges cover-up. Photos are especially powerful.

Validate the target: show the positive aspects of whoever is attacked.

People who are tortured need to be shown to be human. Photos and personal details help to make targets seem like other people and challenge degrading labels or mental images.

Interpret the events as unjust.

Information can be provided about what is actually happening (to counter lies), about the damaging effects of torture (to counter minimisation), about who is really responsible (to counter blaming) and about the damage caused by torture as well as its low value for obtaining information (to counter framing).

Mobilise support. Avoid or discredit official channels.

Mobilising support means getting more people to see things your way, join your campaigns, and protest against torture. This is the primary way to use outrage to challenge injustice. Because official channels usually dampen outrage, it is better to avoid them, or at least not to rely on them.

After the 1986 accident at the Chernobyl nuclear power plant, the Soviet government used various techniques to decrease outrage, but was largely unsuccessful.

Resist intimidation and rewards.

Some people need to stand up in the face of intimidation, for example by speaking out about torture. Also useful is documenting and exposing intimidation: this can arouse greater outrage and contribute to backfire. Likewise, some people need to resist the temptation of getting a reward.

Using these five types of methods increases the likelihood that attacks will backfire. However, the outcome of the struggle depends on a wide range of factors.

The backfire model is a guide to the likely tactics used by powerful perpetrators of injustice to decrease outrage and the sorts of counter-tactics that can increase outrage. It describes tactics and counter-tactics, but what actually happens depends on the circumstances, the people involved and decisions made.

What's not included in the model

- Choice of methods. Should more effort be put into exposing injustice or to countering devaluation, or something else? Decisions about what method to use need to be made by the people involved, based on the circumstances.

- Timing. When is the best time to expose an injustice? Probably not when the media are preoccupied with some natural disaster or celebrity story, or when the movement is not ready to take advantage of outrage. Choosing the right time is crucially important.

- Local knowledge. People who are deeply involved with an issue know an incredible amount about history, social dynamics, arguments, personalities and much else. The model provides only a general framework. Local knowledge is vital to provide insight into what to do and when to do it.

- Culture and values. What people consider just or unjust depends on their culture and prevailing values. The model is based on the way things are now — the current set of beliefs and behaviours. If people's beliefs about injustice change, a process sometimes influenced by campaigning, then the basis for outrage will change.

- Long-term change. The model deals with reactions to actions. It doesn't address how to bring about change in the longer term.

How the model can help

- Many activists think mainly about what they are going to do, such as hold a rally or start a campaign. The backfire model draws attention to what opponents will do, in particular the tactics powerful opponents will use to reduce outrage over injustice.

- Some activists think official channels provide a solution. For example, they sometimes campaign to get the government to set up an inquiry. The model points to the shortcomings of official channels, especially the way they dampen outrage.

- Activists often believe that injustice automatically creates outrage. For example, if police beat protesters or the government breaks the law, activists think everyone will see how unfair this is. The model shows that powerful perpetrators can use a wide range of techniques that reduce outrage.

2. Backfire analysis

Something bad has happened, such as sexual harassment, unfair dismissal, an environmental disaster, or mass killing. Backfire analysis is a way of examining the struggle over how people react.

People often react to bad things by being concerned, angry, disgusted, upset or outraged.[1] I will mostly use the word "outrage" but the other descriptions may be just as relevant.

In backfire analysis, the focus is on tactics. Tactics are actions; they are things that people do. In backfire analysis, it's not so important to explain why things happen.

In looking at tactics, the focus is on how outrage is increased or reduced.

Why would you want to undertake a backfire analysis? After all, the event has already occurred and there's nothing that can be done about it. First, an analysis can provide insight into tactics used by perpetrators, to learn how they operate and thus be better prepared for the next time. Second, a backfire analysis can be used to raise people's awareness about the way struggles over outrage occur — it can provide insight. Third, a backfire analysis can change the way people react to issues: it can make them angry or increase their resolve. As they learn about the techniques used by powerful perpetrators — especially about intimidation, cover-up and devaluation — they may become more sympathetic to the targets of attack.

---

[1] Sometimes people's reactions are closer to apathy or despair, which are not so useful for opposing the bad thing.

In this chapter, I tell about how to undertake a backfire analysis. The first topic is collecting information: I give three examples of how this can be done. Then I look at classifying tactics under the categories of cover-up, devaluation, reinterpretation, official channels, and intimidation/rewards. Finally, I tell about ways to write a backfire story.

Collecting information

To undertake a backfire analysis, you need lots of information. This could be from books, articles, blogs, interviews and personal observations. Let's say you want to analyse the tactics used at a large rally where police assaulted and arrested protesters. You can obtain news reports, blogs, photos, and interview material — anything that provides information. If the rally was in 1915, you'll have to rely entirely on archival documents, as no one who was there is still alive. However, perhaps there are cMy children or grandchildren or others who heard stories of the event.

If the rally occurred recently, you can talk with people who were there. That's a massive job. There might be hundreds or even thousands of people. Likewise, if the rally was a major news item, there might be hundreds of media stories. You don't need to obtain every possible bit of information — just enough. I'll come back to this.

If possible, you should obtain information from both sides: the protesters and the police. So search police media releases, news stories quoting police, police newsletters and consider interviewing police. Getting information from different perspectives provides much greater insight into tactics used. Furthermore, by using a range of sources, your analysis will have more credibility.

Sometimes there are multiple sides. Maybe politicians or media commentators have different views than protesters or police. Here are three examples of how I collected information for a backfire analysis.

Example 1: Rodney King

On 3 March 1991, Los Angeles police arrested a man named Rodney King, who had been driving while drunk and fleeing police in pursuit. In the course of the arrest, the police used tasers against King and hit him with metal batons dozens of times. The beating was recorded on videotape by a witness in a nearby apartment and later shown on television, leading to a massive backlash against the police.

Still from the video of the beating of Rodney King

I decided to investigate the King beating as an example of backfire. Because the case was so prominent, I assumed there would be plenty of material showing techniques for reducing and promoting outrage — and I was right. I obtained about ten books dealing with the beating, some from the police side, some from King's side and some not taking a strong position. There are also some good articles. I read through the books, taking notes whenever I came across instances of methods affecting outrage. For example, I read about the "police code of silence," an unwritten rule that officers never report on abuses by fellow officers. I found out that 20 police were present at the arrest, but not a single one reported any problem. This fitted the category of cover-up. The police code of silence meant that none of the 20 police was likely to reveal what they saw, even if they thought the beating was too harsh.

Because there was so much printed material, I decided not to seek interviews. After all, journalists and investigators had already interviewed all the key people, sometimes in great depth, so I could rely on their accounts. Sometimes there were minor discrepancies between what different sources said, so I had to decide what to say, if anything, about these points.[2]

Example 2: The dismissal of Ted Steele

In 2001, Ted Steele, a tenured associate professor in biology, was dismissed from the University of Wollongong — where I work. Steele had been commenting to the media about "soft marking," namely giving some students higher grades than they deserved. The Vice-Chancellor, without warning, fired Steele. This created enormous media attention, with Steele being defended on free speech grounds. The dismissal produced much extensive bad publicity for the university over a lengthy period: it backfired.

Normally I prefer not to analyse cases at any organisation where I'm personally involved. It's better if an outsider does it, because they can approach the issues in a more balanced way and have more credibility due to being independent. However, despite the extensive coverage of the dismissal and subsequent court proceedings, no one undertook an in-depth analysis, so I decided to write an article about the case, in part to defend the Department of Biological Sciences, caught in the cross-fire between Steele's allegations and the uproar over his dismissal.

I decided not to conduct interviews, as there was plenty of published material about the events. As an academic at the university, I did have one advantage: access to emails going back years, from Steele and others, in particular about Steele's challenges to the university administration. Also, I attended a crucial meeting of the local branch of the National Tertiary Education Union — covering academics across Australia — at which the issue of supporting Steele was discussed. (Many of Steele's

---

2   Brian Martin, "The beating of Rodney King: the dynamics of backfire," *Critical Criminology*, Vol. 13, No. 3, 2005, pp. 307–326.

colleagues in Biological Sciences did not want to support him.) After my letter about the dismissal was published in a newspaper, more people talked to me about the case, and I picked up information from a number of them. I always checked claims with more than one person.

After I wrote a draft of my article, I sent it to all key players, including Steele, the Vice-Chancellor, members of Biological Sciences, and union officials. Only some of them replied; feedback from those who did allowed me to modify a few points. Because the case was current, I needed to be extra careful in what I said.[3]

Example 3: Freedom Flotilla to Gaza, 2010

In May 2010, a flotilla of six ships set out to deliver humanitarian supplies to Gaza, challenging the Israeli government's blockade. Israeli commandoes attacked the flotilla, killing nine

---

3   Brian Martin, "Boomerangs of academic freedom," *Workplace: A Journal for Academic Labor*, Vol. 6, No. 2, June 2005, http://www.bmartin.cc/pubs/05workplace.html.

passengers and detaining the rest. Many were injured, including some commandoes. The attack on the flotilla generated news coverage around the world and was a massive public relations disaster for the Israeli government.

Most of the commentary was about what happened and whether it was justified. I decided to write a short backfire analysis to highlight the tactics used by the Israeli government to decrease outrage. There was plenty of detailed media coverage to rely on, plus online materials from flotilla members. I didn't try to read it all — that would have taken too long, because I wanted to finish in weeks rather than months. My analysis undoubtedly could have been improved by gaining more information from Israeli sources and from flotilla participants. However, there was more than enough information for my purposes: a short, quick analysis.[4]

Information and its quality

To make a backfire analysis, you need information about what happened. That's not always easy. In high profile cases, like the beating of Rodney King or the attack on the flotilla, there is a lot of public information. In other cases — arrest of a local activist, for example — there may not be much information unless you talk to people involved. And maybe the police won't want to talk with you or give you any information.

Even if you obtain some information, you need to judge its quality. People will lie to you, hide crucial information and sometimes try to discourage you from commenting, for example by threatening to sue for defamation. They might produce elaborate stories that confuse and distort matters. So when you gather information, you need to take the usual precautions of a researcher or investigative journalist: judge the quality of the evidence, assess the credibility of the source and obtain information from multiple independent sources. As you start to put

---

[4] Brian Martin, "Flotilla tactics: how an Israeli attack backfired," *Truthout*, 27 July 2010.

together a story, you may want to probe further into some issues, especially concerning cover-up and intimidation, where deception and distortion are most likely.

Taking sides

You need to be prepared for incredibly strong viewpoints, passionately expressed, sometimes conflicting on basic points. For example, the 1994 Rwandan genocide is often presented as a mass killing of Tutsis by Hutus. However, many "moderate" Hutus were also killed: the killing wasn't just based on ethnicity: politics was also involved. Then there is the complication of killings by the Tutsi-led Rwandan Patriotic Front. Some sup-

Deep gashes delivered by the killers are visible in the skulls that fill one room at the Murambi School.

porters of the RPF are disturbed by any suggestion of killings by Tutsis.

These sorts of differences mean that backfire analysis cannot be neutral. You can decide to focus on methods used by the Rwandan government during the genocide that decrease outrage,[5] or you might decide to look at ways used by the RPF to decrease outrage about atrocities committed by its members. Or you could do both. Even if you do both, you might end up with an unbalanced analysis because more information is available about one side's actions than the other's, or because one side's atrocities are significantly worse than the other's.

The 9/11 attacks can be analysed as a backfire process. The

My Lai Masacre In 1968 during the Indochina war, US troops killed hundreds of Vietnamese civilians in the village of My Lai. Covered up for a year, the massacre eventually generated a huge adverse public reaction against the US government and its war policy.

al Qaeda terrorists did very little to discourage outrage. Their attack was out in the open: there was little cover-up about the action, though some about responsibility for it. Al Qaeda had little capacity to devalue the victims and hardly any prospect of using official channels. After 9/11, Al Qaeda had little capacity for further intimidation. On the other hand, the bombing of Afghanistan, a reprisal action initiated in October 2001, six weeks after 9/11, killed thousands of civilians but generated hardly any outrage in the west compared to 9/11.[6] When you undertake a

---

5   This is what I did in "Managing outrage over genocide: case study Rwanda," *Global Change, Peace & Security,* Vol. 21, No. 3, 2009, pp. 275–290.
6   Brendan Riddick, "The bombing of Afghanistan: the convergence of media and

backfire analysis, you make a choice: look at 9/11, the bombing of Afghanistan — or something else.

Classifying methods

The five methods — cover-up, devaluation, reinterpretation, official channels and intimidation/rewards — are a convenient way to classify possible ways of decreasing outrage. There is nothing sacred about the five methods: they sometimes overlap, and they can be broken down into sub-methods. However, it can be useful to think through the differences between them.

Cover-up is anything that prevents people becoming aware that something is happening. It can also be called hiding or disguising.

At least 10 Afghan civilians, including eight schoolchildren, have been killed in fighting involving Western troops in Narang district of Kunar Province in Afghanistan 27 December 2009.

Cover-up is often the most effective way to prevent outrage. If no one knows about a murder, no one can become upset. For many abuses, cover-up is the initial method used, and it may be so effective that other methods aren't needed. However, if cover-up is unsuccessful, attackers may then use other techniques.

Cover-up is in relation to audiences. For example, journalists might know about political corruption, but if the mass media do not report the story, then the corruption has been covered up in relation to the general public.

Censorship is not quite the same as cover-up: censorship is actively preventing access to information or something else, usually by some law or policy (though sometimes censorship is secret: the existence of censorship is covered up). Cover-up can occur by means other than censorship.

For example, many police beatings are unknown to the police.[7] The police involved do not tell anyone except perhaps other police, who maintain secrecy. The victims of the beatings might not tell anyone because of embarrassment or because they are afraid of further police harassment or assaults (this is the tactic of intimidation). When journalists hear about beatings, they may not report them because they accept the point of view of the police (this is the reinterpretation tactic of framing). There is no official censorship of police beatings, but information about them is restricted. This is a type of de facto cover-up: it happens through a combination of processes.

Devaluation is lowering the status or opinion of a person, group or object. Prejudices, such as racism or sexism, are forms of devaluation, sometimes deeply embedded in a culture. Devaluing can also be an active process, for example labelling someone as a deviant, criminal or terrorist. Another way to devalue some-

---

7 Regina G. Lawrence, *The Politics of Force: Media and the Construction of Police Brutality* (Berkeley: University of California Press, 2000); Charles J. Ogletree, Jr., Mary Prosser, Abbe Smith, and William Talley, Jr.; Criminal Justice Institute at Harvard Law School for the National Association for the Advancement of Colored People, *Beyond the Rodney King Story: An Investigation of Police Misconduct in Minority Communities* (Boston: Northeastern University Press, 1995).

one is by spreading damaging information, for example about membership in an unpopular organisation.

The function of devaluation is to make the target seem unworthy, so that whatever is done to them doesn't seem so bad. Some people will think it's okay to beat or jail a terrorist, so it can be effective to say that opponents are terrorists, even if they are really better described as protesters or environmental activists.

Devaluation is widely used, even when backfire is not likely. Unemployed people are called lazy and women who are raped are called sluts. These are examples of blaming the victim.[8] Protesters are called rabble, rent-a-crowd, malcontents, criminals or terrorists.

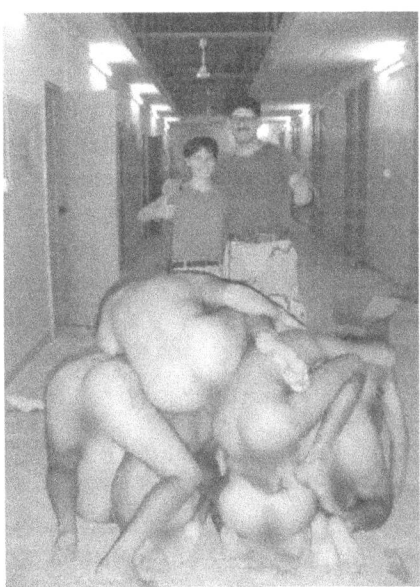

One of the Abu Ghraib photos

---

8   Blaming the victim has a long history. The classic treatment is William Ryan, *Blaming the Victim* (New York: Vintage, 1972).

Reinterpretation is describing an injustice in a different way, so that it doesn't seem so bad or maybe not an injustice at all. There are many ways to do this, so it's convenient to use several classifications: lying, minimising, blaming and framing.

Lying is a direct way of misleading people. A famous lie was the claim, before the 2003 invasion of Iraq, that there was strong evidence Saddam Hussein had nuclear weapons and links to al Qaeda.

Often there's a close link between lying and cover-up. When something isn't ever mentioned at all, this can be part of a cover-up. The US government's lies about Saddam Hussein involved covering up some information, such as intelligence reports. The lies serve as reinterpretation because many people were opposing an invasion and contesting the US government's justifications.

Strictly speaking, a person is lying only if they are consciously aware of deceiving others. There are two main types of lies. One is not revealing the truth, sometimes called lying by omission. The other is telling a falsehood. When someone is convinced what they are saying is true, it's not a lie, even if everyone else thinks it's wrong. When President George W. Bush suggested that Saddam Hussein had nuclear weapons and links to al Qaeda, did he actually believe what he was saying? It's hard to say for sure. However, when classifying tactics, falsehoods like this fit into the category of reinterpretation.

Minimising is saying things aren't as bad as you might think. For example, after the Dili massacre — at which hundreds were killed — Indonesian government officials said 19 people had died. Later they raised this to 50. The actual figure, according to an independent inquiry, was 271.

Sometimes minimising is a type of lying, one that distorts the truth in a direction preferred by the attacker. Like lying, minimising is different from cover-up. The Indonesian government initially tried to prevent any information about the Dili massacre getting to the outside world: it tried to cover up. Its statement about 19 deaths only came after claims about a massacre had been made, and therefore fits the category of reinterpretation better.

Another sort of minimising is in descriptions of torture techniques, saying they are not really so bad. Commentators might say that sleep deprivation is not really all that hurtful or harmful.

Blaming is saying that someone else did it or should be held responsible. Attackers often try to blame the victims. When police beat protesters, the police may claim the protesters attacked them. This overlaps with the tactic of devaluation.

A different sort of blaming occurs when lots of people become outraged over an injustice. Some of those being held responsible may try to blame others involved. After the 1991 beating of Rodney King was broadcast on national television, Los Angeles police chief Daryl Gates blamed the police who made the arrest. Some of these police in turn blamed Gates.

Usually it's easier for powerful figures to blame lower-level functionaries. After the torture of prisoners at Abu Ghraib in Iraq was exposed in 2004, the US government blamed the prison officers involved. No senior US officials were charged with offences, even though it could be argued that they were responsible for the policies that allowed or encouraged torture.

Framing is a way of looking at the world. Imagine you are on the outside of a house, looking in through a small window. Your view depends on the window: you look through the window frame. Someone else looks inside the same house through a different window and gets a different impression, because they are looking from a different direction, into a different room, and perhaps their window has glass that colours or distorts the view.

Framing contests occur when different people look at the same thing — such as the house — from different perspectives. People say their frame is the correct one.

Consider a protest march. The protesters see themselves as expressing their viewpoints and exercising free speech. Government leaders, on the other hand, see the protesters as a dangerous threat to social order and to the government's legitimate role as policy maker. The protesters use a frame of participation and free speech, whereas the government uses a frame of social order and social control.

When police assault a protester, the protesters see this as police brutality. The police look at it entirely differently: they are doing their job to stop threats to public order and violations of the law, and following procedures.

Frames are incredibly powerful and help explain why people believe what they believe and act the way they do. Activists sometimes assume that police or politicians are cynical, corrupt and evil because "they couldn't possibly believe what they're doing is right." The trouble is, they could indeed believe it, and probably do, because they see things using a different perspective.

When politicians start off believing they are right — because they have inside information and are convinced they have the best interests of the country at heart — they then believe they have a responsibility to protect society from dangerous threats. Protesters are seen as a dangerous threat, so for politicians it become legitimate to put protesters under surveillance, pass repressive laws and use heavy police powers. From their perspective, lying is legitimate because it serves a greater purpose, devaluation of protesters is just telling the truth and intimidation is justified because protesters are seen as threatening enemies.

Framing, when based on sincere belief, is the only reinterpretation technique that can be considered legitimate. After all, people should be able to believe what they like, even if they end up with a distorted view of the world. It is legitimate to hold a belief, but problems arise if you try to impose that belief on others or to promote it through techniques such as lying and intimidation.

In 1984, a leak in a chemical plant in India killed thousands and injured hundreds of thousands of people. The owner of the plant, the US-based company Union Carbide, used numerous techniques to reduce public outrage.

Official channels include grievance procedures, expert panels, appeals to politicians, ombudsmen, official investigations, and courts. Official channels can also be called formal procedures. Official channels are processes that are supposed to provide justice, fairness or truth.

In some cases, official channels work just as they are supposed to. A person commits a crime like murder, is arrested, tried and sentenced. Justice is seen to be done.

However, when a government, powerful corporation or military commits a crime, official channels may not work so well: they may give only the appearance of fairness. Because many people believe official channels dispense justice, outrage declines even though justice has *not* been done.

The role of official channels in reducing outrage is the most counter-intuitive feature of the backfire model. Activists often demand government action: they call for an inquiry into poverty or prison violence. They may initiate court cases, for example against police brutality or nuclear power.

Sometimes using official channels is a good option. The backfire model doesn't say never to use them. What it says is that official channels tend to reduce outrage over injustice, largely because so many people believe that if some official body is dealing with the problem, they don't need to be so concerned about it themselves.

Official channels also dampen outrage in other ways.

- They are slow. Inquiries and court cases can take months or even years. During this time, people's initial passions may die down, and other issues arise, competing for attention.

- They are procedural. They involve all sorts of detailed rules, regulations and formalities. In court cases, rules of evidence are followed. Often this means that most attention is on technicalities — minor points of procedure — and not on the central injustice.

- They rely on experts. A lot of knowledge and experience is needed to operate effectively using grievance procedures, government inquiries, expert panels and court cases. This means most people are excluded or lose interest. Official channels are low in public participation. They are good way to transform a mass campaign into a struggle between a few experts.

When powerful perpetrators turn to or set up official channels, like inquiries into massacres, they are moving the issue from the public arena into a different arena: law or bureaucracy. Campaigners need to be aware of this.

Powerful perpetrators prefer official channels they can influence or control. They prefer internal inquiries, not independent inquiries: they would rather have the police investigate police brutality than set up an independent inquiry. They prefer closed inquiries, not open public inquiries: they would rather have courts closed to journalists than run an open court. They typically try to establish terms of reference — namely, the topics the inquiry is supposed to deal with — that are narrow, so the potential impact will be reduced.

The trouble is that closed internal inquiries with narrow terms of reference don't have as much credibility. So sometimes governments set up open, independent, wide-ranging inquiries and hope for the best.

On some rare occasions, an inquiry becomes a form of campaigning. In the mid 1990s in the Australian state of New South Wales, there was a royal commission into police . The commission held public hearings that generated massive news coverage. Even more dramatically, a few corrupt police turned informants and gathered video evidence of deals. Broadcast on television, this made it impossible for the government to avoid taking serious reform measures.[9]

However, for every campaigning commission like this, there are dozens of others that are far tamer. Some of them operate in secrecy or with minimal publicity, so there is little pressure for change. Some of them produce findings that reaffirm the government's position. Yet others generate enlightened and progressive recommendations, which is fine, except that governments never implement them.

When analysing the role of official channels in relation to public outrage, it's useful to think of a wide range of organisations and processes that can serve as official channels. For example, seeking support from a politician can serve as an official channel, especially if the politician promises to help but doesn't deliver or takes a long time. An election is a type of official channel: it gives legitimacy to the system of government. That's why many dictators run elections. Even when they are fraudulent and staged, they can give the appearance, at least to some people, of legitimacy.[10]

9   Rodney Tiffen, *Scandals: Media, Politics and Corruption in Contemporary Australia* (Sydney: University of New South Wales Press, 1999).
10   Benjamin Ginsberg, *The Consequences of Consent: Elections, Citizen Control and Popular Acquiescence* (Reading, MA: Addison-Wesley, 1982).

Intimidation is any threat or attack that discourages the expression of outrage. A government employee would like to speak out about corruption but is afraid of reprisals such as dismissal. A journalist would like to write about corruption but the editor or publisher is afraid of being sued. A victim of police brutality might wish to speak out but is afraid of additional police harassment.

Intimidation is somewhat different from the other tactics, which are designed to reduce outrage; intimidation doesn't necessarily reduce the feeling of outrage, but instead discourages people from acting on their feelings.

In some cases, intimidation is both the attack and the means of deterring the expression of outrage. When police beat protesters, this can cause outrage but at the same time frighten some protesters from exposing what happened.

Some forms of intimidation are overt and obvious, like beatings and shootings. Others are more subtle, such as a menacing look, a hint of a legal action, or police photographers at a rally.

For perpetrators, intimidation has one big disadvantage: it can cause additional outrage. Imagine a journalist reporting on a protest. If the journalist is threatened, beaten or arrested, this can lead the journalist to make greater efforts to expose the issues, as happened in East Timor in 1991 and with the Gaza flotilla in 2010. The same sort of thing can happen when police threaten or hurt protesters, many of whom have the technology and skills to publicise abuses.

Because intimidation is widely seen as wrong, it is often hidden. Police do not announce they are going to harass someone they have beaten. Intimidation often goes hand in hand with cover-up.

Rewards are any sort of benefit, incentive or bribe that makes people less likely to express outrage. Lawyers who worked for McDonald's prosecuting the defamation action against Helen Steel and Dave Morris were amply rewarded for their work.

It can be very difficult to find evidence of this sort of effect.

There is little evidence that any Los Angeles police felt any outrage over the beating of Rodney King, so it's impossible to know whether potential rewards made any difference to their behaviour. Likewise, it's hard to know whether lawyers working for McDonald's thought the McLibel defamation case was misguided. Lawyers regularly work on cases they don't believe in, and typically think this is part of their job.

Rewards are a parallel process to intimidation. The idea with both methods is that people might feel outrage but are potentially discouraged from expressing it, by fear of the consequences (intimidation) or the promise of some benefit (rewards). That's the reason these two methods are grouped together in the backfire model as one category. It would be quite okay to separate them.

Because it's so hard to find solid evidence of rewards, often it's easier not to mention them in a backfire analysis. Intimidation is more obvious because it's directed at the target of the attack and at allies of the target, whereas allies of the perpetrator receive the incentives.

There are a few cases of bribery of targets. Whistleblowers — people who speak out in the public interest — are often met with reprisals such as harassment, reprimands, ostracism, demotion and dismissal. These reprisals are a potential source of outrage. When whistleblowers go to court for unfair dismissal or to obtain compensation, they may receive a settlement offer: a payout. A common condition of the settlement is that the whistleblower sign an agreement not to comment publicly about the settlement or the original issue. To get the money, the whistleblower has to keep quiet. It's a type of bribe.

Sometimes the benefit from remaining a bystander or tacit collaborator is simply to be left alone. Employees who see corrupt behaviour often say nothing because they know there might be repercussions if they do. The "reward" of being left alone can also be seen in terms of the tactic of intimidation: employees are afraid of reprisals. This suggests the close connection that sometimes occurs between intimidation and rewards.

When targets reduce outrage

Tactics that reduce outrage are most commonly used by perpetrators and their allies. Torturers keep quiet about their work and so do governments. But sometimes victims contribute. Victims of torture are often highly traumatised and fearful. They may not feel safe enough to speak out about their experiences. When they remain silent, they contribute to cover-up.

It would be absurd to blame torture victims for cover-up. When doing a backfire analysis, the purpose is to understand the processes that contribute to greater outrage. Because torture victims have been subject to extreme intimidation, others may need to speak on their behalf.

Workers who have been bullied on the job often feel humiliated and violated. Sometimes they begin to believe what everyone else seems to believe, that they are responsible for what is happening to them. The result is that many bullied workers are unwilling to tell others about their experiences, or perhaps are

Terrorists often use methods that increase public opposition to the activities.

willing to tell only friends and not anyone else. They can be said to be contributing to cover-up. This is perfectly understandable and the greatest care is needed when suggesting to bullied workers that they speak out.

Many people believe in the power of official channels to dispense justice. Bullied workers often make complaints to their bosses and higher managers, make formal grievances, or go to court. Sometimes these appeals are effective; in many cases, though, they are worse than nothing. Appeal processes can involve attempts to discredit the worker that are experienced like a continuation of the bullying.[11]

In terms of the backfire model, the key point is that using official channels is likely to dampen outrage. If the goal is to mobilise support, then it's often better to avoid official channels or use them as a tool in campaigning. However, not everyone understands how powerful it can be to mobilise support; some of those who do understand may want to use official channels anyway.

The key point here is that targets of injustice sometimes con-

---

11 Deborah Osborne, "Pathways into bullying," Proceedings of the 4th Asia Pacific Conference on Educational Integrity, Wollongong, 2009, http://ro.uow.edu.au/apcei/09/papers/18/.

tribute to reducing outrage. Often there are good reasons for this that should be respected. Sometimes, though, targets do not realise they are playing into the hands of perpetrators.

When perpetrators increase outrage

According to the backfire model, powerful perpetrators of injustice can use various methods that reduce outrage over their actions. But sometimes attackers seem to ignore these methods or even do the exact opposite — they do things that increase outrage!

Beginning in 2002, President George W. Bush and other senior US officials signalled their intentions to launch an invasion of Iraq. An illegal, aggressive war was likely to trigger opposition, but rather than hide their plans, they trumpeted them widely. This helped to stimulate a massive resistance, of which the most dramatic moment was the largest protest gathering in history on 15 February 2003, with millions of people in the streets in cities around the world.

This can be contrasted with the approach used by US President Ronald Reagan in the 1980s, when military aggression against the government and people of Nicaragua was disguised. The US government, rather than directly attacking Nicaragua, provided covert assistance to the Contras. This partial cover-up of the aggression meant that it was much harder to generate opposition.

Sometimes attackers are quite open about their actions and motivations because they believe there is no significant opposition or because they are arrogant and think they can do what they like, or because they need to mobilise support for their approach. Some open attacks serve as a powerful form of intimidation.

Then there is terrorism: attacks on civilians as a means of sending a message to audiences.[12] Terrorists have different aims.

---

12 On this communication model of terrorism, see Alex P. Schmid and Janny de Graaf, *Violence as Communication: Insurgent Terrorism and the Western News Media* (London: Sage, 1982). See also Brigitte L. Nacos, *Mass-Mediated Terrorism: The Cen-*

World Trade Center Attacked September 11 2001

Some seek revenge for previous injustices. Some seek attention to their cause through dramatic actions. Others are more strategic: they hope to trigger a reaction from their targets — for example, increased repression — that is so strong that it will mobilise greater support for their cause, namely backfire in their favour.

Whatever the rationale, terrorist actions seem designed to maximise outrage. Think of 9 September 2001: the attacks on civilians were in broad daylight, enabling maximum publicity; they were not hidden. The attackers had little capacity to devalue their targets or to use official channels or intimidation against their opponents. The result: a giant backfire in the form of popular support for the US government and people, the bombing of Afghanistan and a massive expansion of the US security system.

The lesson: do not assume perpetrators always do everything possible to reduce outrage. Inadvertently or on purpose, they sometimes do the exact opposite.

---

tral Role of the Media in Terrorism and Counterterrorism (Lanham, MD: Rowman & Littlefield, 2002); Joseph S. Tuman, *Communicating Terror: The Rhetorical Dimensions of Terrorism* (Thousand Oaks, CA: Sage, 2003).

Writing a backfire story

You've collected material about tactics used in a case of injustice. You have information about cover-up, devaluation and so forth. You're ready to write the story. How should you organise the material?

1. Story, then analysis[13]

You first tell the story of what happened, for example background, the massacre and the consequences, giving all relevant details as you go along. After telling the story, you point out the tactics used, first cover-up, then devaluation and so forth.

This approach has the advantage of allowing a full narrative, uninterrupted by references to theory as you go along. It's also fairly easy to write. The disadvantage is that readers may not be able to hold the full narrative in their heads, so when you get to the analysis of tactics, they may not remember relevant details.

2. Story with analysis along the way[14]

You construct the story so that you can do the analysis of tactics as you go. You might start describing those elements of the story involving cover-up, then devaluation and so on. Sometimes a brief summary of events at the beginning is helpful.

This construction provides both a narrative and vivid links to tactics. However, it can be challenging to tell the story this way. You might need to backtrack on the time sequence or refer to key events more than once.

3. Analysis illustrated by examples[15]

You systematically describe the tactics used. For each tactic — cover-up, etc. — you use a variety of examples. In analysing tactics used with torture, you might use examples from different places and times.

---

13 Examples are chapters 2, 3 and 4 of *Justice Ignited*.
14 Examples are chapters 5, 8, 9 and 10 of *Justice Ignited*.
15 Examples are chapters 6, 11 and 12 of *Justice Ignited*.

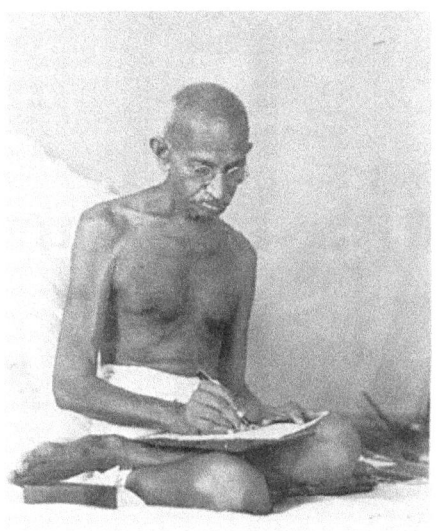

Mohandas Gandhi wrote almost every day. His collected works are 100 volumes.

This approach highlights the analysis while retaining the power of examples. It lacks the power of narrative and potentially can be criticised as picking examples to suit the analysis.

There's no ideal way to write about backfire. These are three general approaches; there are many others. How to proceed depends on your audience, your material and your purpose. A lengthy academic treatment will be quite different in tone and structure to a short treatment aimed at activists.

Writing: how to go about it

Most researchers collect lots of information, taking notes along the way, and then sit down to write about what they've found. This can work well with small projects but becomes increasingly dysfunctional when there is lots of material.

An alternative approach is to start writing the article from

the beginning, based on what you already know, and to add to it bit by bit. Robert Boice in his studies with writers and academics found that those who did small amounts of writing each day, day after day, had much higher productivity than those who didn't write anything until prodded into a burst of frenzied effort, often because of a deadline.[16] Writing to deadlines can be called bingeing. It feels so stressful that you don't want to repeat it very soon.

To use Boice's approach, you should write a little bit on the article each day, maybe writing new text for 5 to 20 minutes and then spending a similar period editing what you've already written. When you come to something you don't already know, leave a note to yourself about what you need to look up.

The advantage is that your mind works through the rest of the day, mostly unconsciously, dealing with the issues and helping you put them into a logical framework. You save time because instead of reading vast quantities before writing, your daily writing provides a framework. You don't need to read as

---

16 Robert Boice, *Advice for New Faculty Members: Nihil Nimus* (Boston: Allyn and Bacon, 2000).

much because you know what you're looking for.

When you finish a first draft and have gone over it to polish it, it's time to obtain comments. Tara Gray, who turned Boice's approach into a programme for publishing,[17] recommends sending your draft first to non-experts, people who don't know a lot about the topic. Suppose you're writing about tactics used by the US government that decrease outrage from the bombing of Afghanistan beginning in October 2001. First you show your draft paper to people who haven't studied the Afghanistan war and who are unfamiliar with the backfire model. They will make comments and ask questions that help you to clarify your argument. For example, they might ask how you know there were civilian casualties or what you mean by official channels.

After you make changes based on the comments from non-experts, next send your article to experts in the area, if possible to experts in the topic area — the bombing of Afghanistan — and experts on backfire tactics. They will be able to comment on facts and interpretations.

Why bother sending your article to non-experts? Surely the experts know best! The trouble is that experts are so familiar with the subject matter that they may not notice that you haven't explained concepts clearly or organised your material logically. The experts already know the concepts and may not notice problems in exposition because the content is obvious to them.

Most of your readers will probably be non-experts, so you need to communicate to them. However, if you make mistakes, you can lose credibility, especially if there are critics of your analysis. You need input from experts to help make your treatment more accurate.

The combination of regular writing and seeking feedback on drafts from non-experts and experts can result in a highly effective piece of writing. The more you write, the better you get, as long as you keep trying to improve.

---

17   Tara Gray, *Publish & Flourish: Become a Prolific Scholar* (Teaching Academy, New Mexico State University, 2005).

Publishing

Where should you publish your backfire analysis? This depends on your intended audience and your purpose.

Your primary audience might be activists, members of a particular organisation, or anyone interested. Thinking about your intended audience is important, because it should influence the language you use, the amount of information, the length and appearance of your publication.

Academic articles can be useful for providing detailed documentation and rigorous argument. But usual academic style of writing is seldom appealing for non-specialists (or even for specialists!). So if you want to reach a broader readership, you can write something that is shorter, tells a story, provides plenty of examples and is clearly expressed. You can find good examples on websites for political commentary.

An article is one option. You can also consider a slide show, a radio programme, a video or a poster. You can think of different formats, such as a debate, a diary or a mystery.

The way to proceed depends on your purpose. You may want to inform audiences, for example to help activists think about how to be more effective, or to alert members of the public to an important issue. You may want to contribute to a greater understanding of the issue or of the process of backfire. You may want to develop your skills in analysis, writing, publishing or interaction with audiences. The more you produce, the more you develop your skills and the more effective you can be in raising awareness.

3. Preparing

You're planning to do something and there's a chance of being attacked. What should you do? The backfire model can provide guidance.

- You work for a company and have discovered evidence of corruption. You're thinking of speaking out about it.
- You're planning a rally and are concerned about the possibility of police violence.
- Your group has taken a leading role in opposing a powerful politician. You're worried about reprisals.

In cases like these, you need to think through possible risks and plan accordingly. You want to prepare so that you're less likely to be attacked and so that, if you are attacked, it might backfire on the attacker.

The way to go about this is to start by thinking of what your opponent might do — namely, attack — and what the opponent might do to reduce outrage over the attack. The likely methods are cover-up, devaluation, reinterpretation, official channels and intimidation.

Corruption

You work for a company and have discovered evidence of corruption. You're thinking of speaking out about it.[1]

This is an example of individual action that makes you vulnerable to attack. Similar dynamics are involved in resisting bullying, racism, sexism — any sort of unfairness or abuse that is endorsed or tolerated by managers. You need to look at what opponents might do that reduces outrage, starting with cover-up.

Cover-up

You can predict that the attacker will use some methods to cover up what they do or the responsibility for it. Of course those involved in the corruption try to keep it hidden. As soon as you speak out, they will know they are being exposed and will take further steps to cover up. So think about what they might do.

They might destroy evidence. That means that you need to collect every possible bit of evidence beforehand. It's risky going to the police and asking them to do a raid, because if the corrupt operators get a whiff of the raid, they will destroy documents in advance. They might have contacts in the police.

---

[1] On whistleblowing, see for example C. Fred Alford, *Whistleblowers: Broken Lives and Organizational Power* (Ithaca, NY: Cornell University Press, 2001); Myron Peretz Glazer and Penina Migdal Glazer, *The Whistleblowers: Exposing Corruption in Government and Industry* (New York: Basic Books, 1989); Geoffrey Hunt, ed., *Whistleblowing in the Social Services: Public Accountability and Professional Practice* (London: Edward Arnold, 1998); Marcia P. Miceli and Janet P. Near, *Blowing the Whistle: The Organizational and Legal Implications for Companies and Employees* (New York: Lexington Books, 1992); Terance D. Miethe, *Whistleblowing at Work: Tough Choices in Exposing Fraud, Waste, and Abuse on the Job* (Boulder, CO: Westview, 1999).

Suppose you've collected plenty of evidence. Where have you saved it? A file on your computer? Maybe the corrupt operators will decide to steal your computer or pay someone to steal it, making it look like a regular burglary. So you need to make sure you have back-up copies: full sets of all the evidence in safe keeping with several friends or lawyers.

Andrew Wilkie, an intelligence analyst who in 2003 spoke out about shortcomings of the Australian government's case for joining the invasion of Iraq. The Australian government used various techniques to discredit Wilkie, but he effectively countered them.

Devaluation

If you speak out about corruption — in other words, you become a whistleblower — you might imagine that you will be praised for your courage and commitment. Think again. Those involved with the corruption, or who have tolerated it, would rather reduce outrage. What better way than to discredit you?

So they might spread rumours about you: your poor performance, your sexual behaviour, your frauds and deceits, or your personality disorders. Some rumours might have an element of truth; others might be totally fabricated. They might go through your personnel file, looking for the slightest bit of evidence to hurt your reputation. Perhaps someone complained about you 5 or 10 years ago. That will be publicised and exaggerated into a major flaw. You might be harassed and provoked so that you crack and yell at someone to stop; then the fact that you yelled will be used to discredit you. Every negative aspect of your job evaluations will be trumpeted to anyone who cares to listen.

These things might not happen — but they could. So you need to be prepared. Before you speak out, you need to gather all available evidence of your good performance and pleasant personality. Save copies of all your glowing job evaluations. Obtain statements from your bosses and co-workers. Gather every bit of documentation you can about your good character and be prepared to use it to counter attacks on your credibility.

You need to be prepared for efforts to provoke you into doing something that's seen as inappropriate. That means that when others make nasty comments or do things they know will annoy you, you need to resist the temptation to shout, storm off or make rude comments. Of course you might be completely justified, but this isn't about what's fair, it's about what's effective. To be effective, you need to behave impeccably, better than anyone else. If possible, you need to find others who will speak on your behalf, saying what a conscientious and nice person you are.

Maybe there are a few things you'd rather people didn't know about, maybe a drunken escapade or a time you made a mess of your job. Be prepared for these stories to be made public, much more public than you'd like. If this sort of bad publicity is going to hurt you and your loved ones more than you can handle, then now is the time to reconsider whether to speak out. Are there other options?

One option is to find someone else to speak out, some co-worker who has less to lose. This isn't easy, but it's possible.

Another option is to get another job, in a secure situation with a sympathetic boss, and then speak out. Your old employers — the corrupt ones — might still try to discredit you, but they won't be able to provoke you into unwise behaviours.

Yet another option is to leak documents and remain anonymous. You can find a sympathetic journalist or action group to give the documents to, or, if the issue is big enough, post them on WikiLeaks or another online repository.[2] If you are anonymous, it is much harder to discredit you, and furthermore you remain on the job, able to collect more material. But be prepared for all sorts of efforts to find out who the leaker is. That's a different scenario, requiring careful preparations.

Reinterpretation

You need to be prepared for lies, minimising of what happened, blaming and framing.

Suppose you were at a meeting when the boss asked someone to sign false statements. You might imagine you could report this — after all, there were a dozen witnesses. But then you find that the boss denies asking anyone to sign statements, and every other person there supports the boss. They are all lying! If this is a really big issue, you might prepare by covertly recording the conversation. (Be careful: if your recording is discovered, it may destroy your relationships.) Moral: when others might lie, you need strong documentation. Lying can also be a mode of cover-up.

The boss might say that signing false statements is not a big deal; it goes on all the time. This is the technique of minimising: saying what happened is not as important as others might think. To counter this, you can collect information showing that it is important. Maybe there were previous examples in your own organisation in which signing false statements was treated as a major ethical violation. Another possibility is finding the

---

2   On leaking, see Kathryn Flynn, "The practice and politics of leaking," *Social Alternatives*, Vol. 30, No. 1, 2011, pp. 24–28, http://www.bmartin.cc/pubs/11sa/Flynn.html

way this sort of action is treated in other organisations, especially those with good reputations for probity.

The boss — if caught red-handed doing the wrong thing — might try to blame others. One possibility is blaming the workers who signed the false statement, saying they have responsibility. Another possibility is blaming higher management for requiring this sort of behaviour. You might think it's unfair to blame workers who have to choose between signing false statements and losing their jobs, or you might think they are all to blame. The risk in allowing the blaming game to take hold is that responsibility is diffused and eventually only a few scapegoats suffer any penalty. So be prepared with information and understanding of procedures that enable blame to be assigned correctly.

Finally there is the viewpoint that this is the way things are done: there's nothing really wrong with it because overall no

High Court of Australia

one is hurt, and too much red tape just costs time and bother without any benefit. Or maybe the viewpoint is that this is the way it's always been done, and it's okay. This is a perspective on corruption that it's normal. It's a way of looking at the issue, often held quite sincerely. You have a different viewpoint — a different frame — namely, that signing false statements is wrong. You need to be prepared with evidence and arguments to counter the view that "our actions are okay."

The struggle over interpretations is about the meaning of events. What really happened? How significant is it? Is this normal behaviour or corruption? You need to be prepared to confront others who will present information and views completely different from yours, and who will disguise and distort perceptions and interpretations in a self-serving way.

Official channels

Official channels tend to dampen outrage. So how do you prepare for them? If you decide to make a formal complaint or mount a court action — despite the disadvantages — then find out beforehand about the most promising options. Sometimes you have a choice of official channels: an organisational grievance procedure, an ombudsman, an auditor-general, an anti-corruption commission, a politician or several types of courts, for example. Before embarking on what seems the most obvious and relevant option, find out about it. Who else has used the same method? How long did it take? How much did it cost? Were they successful?

Whistleblowers know their own case intimately and often believe, quite strongly, that they are right. So they think, "Of course the complaint procedure or the court will rule in my favour." That's one reason why whistleblowers keep trying official channels despite their manifest weaknesses. The trouble is, official channels do not operate on the basis of who's right: they operate on the basis of rules and formal processes, and these can sabotage even the most powerful case — powerful on paper, that is.

By finding out about previous experiences with official channels, some realism can be brought into planning. If only 1 out of 50 previous applicants to a court was successful, then your odds are the same: 1 out of 50.[3] Turn off the voice that says "My case

---

3   For some courts, this is close to the actual figure. In the US, which has the longest

is different" because it will send you down a path to destruction. What if there isn't any information about previous experiences? Then ask around to find out who else has tried the same thing. Even one or two previous stories are far better than none.

If you decide to engage with an official channel, be aware of what your opponents will do. They will try to slow down the process, keep everything as confidential as possible, make everything as technical and procedural as they can, and increase your costs. You are hoping for a quick, focused, open process. Good luck, because all the pressures will be in the other direction. Be prepared for a long slog. Assess your finances, your relationships and your supporters. Can you last for months or years? If going to court, are you prepared for appeals, spinning the process out for years?

You may decide instead to avoid official channels and instead mount a campaign. This requires planning too. This is a whole separate topic. It includes writing stories of your experiences, mustering supporting evidence, being prepared to speak, finding allies, making information available, liaising with the media, and much else.[4]

Intimidation

When you do something like speaking out about corruption, you need to be prepared for reprisals. Don't be surprised and taken off balance. Instead, be prepared. Read about what's involved in being "resilient" in the face of adversity.[5]

experience with whistleblower legislation, "Between passage of the 1994 amendments and September 2002, whistleblowers lost 74 of 75 decisions on the merits at the Federal Court of Appeals, which has a monopoly on judicial review of administrative decisions." Tom Devine, "Whistleblowing in the United States: The Gap between Vision and Lessons Learned," in *Whistleblowing around the World: Law, Culture and Practice*, ed. Richard Calland and Guy Dehn (Cape Town: Open Democracy Advice Centre; London: Public Concern at Work, 2004), pp. 74–100, at pp. 83–84.

4   Brian Martin, *The Whistleblower's Handbook: How to Be an Effective Resister* (Charlbury, UK: Jon Carpenter, 1999), http://www.bmartin.cc/pubs/99wh.html.

5   Salvatore R Maddi and Deborah M Khoshaba, *Resilience at Work: How to Succeed no Matter what Life Throws at You* (New York: Amacom, 2005); Amanda Ripley, *The Unthinkable: Who Survives When Disaster Strikes — and Why* (New York: Three Rivers

You should tell your family and close friends what to expect, at least if this information won't distress them too much. If they are prepared, they can support you more effectively.

If some of the reprisals have financial implications, for example if you could lose your job or be sued, take action in advance to reduce the danger. This might mean paying off debts, cutting back on expenses, finding another job, or transferring assets to others.

If there are physical dangers, for example of being assaulted, you need to protect yourself. How to do this depends a lot on the circumstances. It might mean avoiding certain places, checking your car before driving, leaving town or even creating a new identity.

One of the most powerful ways to deal with intimidation is to document and expose it. This is because many people think intimidation is wrong and will support you more if they believe you are being attacked. So be prepared to use all the usual methods of collecting information, but this time in advance of possible reprisals. This might involve collecting emails or signed statements, recording conversations or taking photos. It might involve having contingency plans in case you're arrested, so that others can take action on your behalf.[6]

Press, 2009).

6   Zorana Smiljanic, "Plan B: Using Secondary Protests to Undermine Repression," New Tactics in Human Rights, http://www.newtactics.org/en/PlanB

These precautions might not be necessary and others might think you're being paranoid. Being prepared for attack is still quite sensible even if it seems braver to just wait and handle whatever comes. Being prepared for the worst can make you more confident and able to act: you don't need to worry as much.

If you're well prepared, opponents are actually less likely to attack, if they realise that their attacks will be exposed and potentially backfire. So it's often a good idea to let others know that you're prepared.

Police violence

You're planning a rally and are concerned about the possibility of police violence.

This is an example of attack on a public protest. Attacks might also come from opponents (counter-protesters), vigilantes or paid thugs.

Cover-up

When police use force against protesters, they seldom want witnesses to see what they're doing. If they appear to be brutal, it will look bad to witnesses. Indeed, it is a classic type of unfairness: one person hitting another, who doesn't resist, without justification.

So it's predictable that police and their allies will try to limit visibility concerning police brutality — especially to independent audiences. How can they do this?

One way is to beat protesters out of sight, when they think no one will see or record the violence. Cameras are a way to counter this. The police know this, so they try to confiscate or damage cameras. To prepare for this, lots of protesters should have cameras. Audio recording is another option, to capture what police are saying.

Recording video and audio is the first step. The next is to

make this material available to audiences, with credibility. Videos can be uploaded onto YouTube; they need to be identified so that the events make sense. Then people need to be notified about the YouTube material.

Technology for recording and distributing information is continually developing. Technological details are important and need to be assessed in light of key elements of the challenge to cover-up:

- gather information
- distribute information to audiences
- make it credible

Making information credible can be by involvement of a respected journalist or other observer, by collecting high-quality images and putting them together into a compelling narrative, and by distributing the information through outlets with status or influence.

Sometimes photos are not very revealing. There are ways

Electroshock baton. Governments and companies selling and using equipment for torture use various methods to reduce public outrage.

for police to hurt protesters without appearing so bad, for example pain compliance holds, rubbing pepper spray into eyes, and electroshock batons. To expose these sorts of methods, you need to think about what is credible to an audience. Maybe having several protesters tell about their experiences would be effective. A medical expert could testify about the impact of the methods used.

Occasionally, a member of the police is willing to speak out. However, doing so would probably mean the end of their career. Another option is leaks from within the police, for example notes on police plans or recordings of interrogations. If protesters can cultivate a police insider, this is a powerful way to expose abuse. If the police think a member of the force is divulging information, this might lead to more caution on their part. It might also lead to a witch-hunt for potential leakers.

Discussing witch-hunts for police leakers seems almost a different topic from the original one: cover-up of police brutality and how to counter it. The key point here is not about which particular counter-tactics you choose, but the process of thinking about it. You begin by thinking of what the police might do — beating protesters — and assume they will try to hide their brutality from wider audiences. Then you proceed to think of how to expose the brutality, and what the police might to do stop you exposing it. You need to think creatively. There are no answers that always work, because the police will learn from your actions and you will learn from theirs.

Devaluation

Police can get away with brutality more easily if people think the protesters are lower status. For most people, hurting a criminal, terrorist or disreputable-looking protester who behaves weirdly is not as bad as hurting a valued member of the community.

Therefore, it is predictable that police and others who support the police or oppose the protesters will use the technique of devaluation. They will apply labels: they will call protesters "rabble," "low-life," "rent-a-crowd" or "terrorists." Unsympathetic photographers will show the protesters in the worst possible light, for example through pictures of less conventional protesters in unflattering poses. They will claim protesters were violent. They will dredge up information, for example about previous crimes, bad behaviour, misuse of funds, infighting or racist statements, and use it to discredit the protesters. Some of the information might be misleading or manufactured. The aim is to discredit the protesters.

To be prepared for devaluation tactics, several factors are worth considering.

- Appearance
- Participants
- Behaviour
- Reputation
- Commitments

Many observers judge protesters by the way they appear, even though, in a logical sense, this should have little or nothing to do with the credibility of the protesters' cause. Appearance makes a difference. Slovenly or unorthodox dress can reduce credibility. So think carefully about what image you want to send. Is it about responsible citizens? You may prefer a casual look, to encourage greater participation. An alternative is formal dress, to suggest a higher status. Or everyone could wear the same colour. Or occupational groups, such as nurses or sporting teams, could wear their work uniforms.

Devaluation is harder when participants have high status. So it's worth thinking about who might join. Older people can give the authority of experience and seniority. Prominent individuals — politicians, artists, media personalities — can add glamour. Perhaps some of the protesters have credibility due to their roles as journalists, lawyers, doctors or religious leaders. If individuals with credibility become victims of police brutality, their personal stories will help to validate the protesters, especially with audiences that trust them.

The behaviour of protesters can make a big difference. If protesters have been shouting ugly slogans and shaking their fists, this gives an impression of being angry and aggressive, so it's easier to portray them as violent. On the other hand, if protesters are polite, singing tunefully or having fun, this gives an impression of being positive and happy, an image that is harder to devalue.

Even when just a few protesters behave in a way that can be

discredited — for example, by swearing, making rude signs, throwing rocks or assaulting opponents — this can be used to discredit the entire group. Media often focus on the most violent or outrageous actions, picking a few seconds of conflict as newsworthy and ignoring hours of peaceful behaviour. To avoid this sort of discrediting image-making, protesters need to prepare to resist temptations to behave in ways that can be portrayed negatively. Police know that protester violence is bad for protesters, and may try to provoke protesters through taunts or rough treatment, hoping that some protesters will lose their tempers and strike back. When that happens, police violence is far easier to justify: it is seen as a response to protester violence.

Some police forces go further in their efforts to provoke protesters. They may use agents provocateurs, namely police agents or stooges who pretend to be protesters and act in ways that discredit the protest. Provocateurs sometimes take a lead role in promoting violence, throwing bricks or organising purchase of materials to make explosives. Provocateurs who are more subtle will use their influence to convince or goad others into using violence. The protesters who are dupes of the provocateur think they have made their own decision to use violence, while the provocateur can remain in the background, perhaps fading out of the scene.

The use of agents provocateurs shows that police sometimes prefer protesters to be more aggressive. The reason is image: when protesters use violence, many observers believe that the protesters' goal is aggression and causing harm: the observers look at the methods used and assume that the purpose is similar to the methods. The protesters might be concerned about environmental problems or human rights, but if they use violence, their message can be lost due to the image created. The theory behind this is called correspondent inference theory: observers infer purposes by assuming a correspondence with actions taken.[7] This is a good argument for behaving in ways that are compatible with the goals being sought.

Your reputation can protect you, to some extent, against devaluation. If the group organising the protest is known as responsible, prestigious, predictable and principled, then claims that the group is despicable and criminal are not likely to be believed. Indeed, if your reputation is good enough, attempts at devaluation may be so transparently false that they discredit the attackers.

The next question is how to build a reputation. This isn't easy. Even if the protest includes movie stars and Nobel Prize winners, they can be attacked as dupes of organisers. Often, the best reputation comes from involvement of people who are person-

---

7   Max Abrahms, "Why terrorism does not work," *International Security*, Vol. 31, No. 2, Fall 2006, pp. 42–78.

ally known in the community. If participants include next-door neighbours, family doctors, school teachers and community workers — people who are known personally and respected — then it is likely that their version of the protest will be trusted over claims by critics.

Building a reputation is an ongoing challenge. It is definitely worth the effort.

Another way to resist devaluation is by making commitments. If the organisers say that everyone must remain nonviolent, or participate in nonviolence workshops beforehand, this can increase the credibility of the protest. Commitments are useful, but to be credible, they need to be matched by behaviour.

Reinterpretation

You say that police were brutal and protesters were badly hurt. The police and politicians say that the police never struck anyone, that protesters were violent, that protesters' injuries were minor, that protester complaints have no substance, that a few rogue police were responsible for injuries, that police were just doing their duty, and that law and order must be maintained.

If police assault protesters, you can predict these sorts of lies, justifications and rationalisations. The police will lie about what happened, minimise its significance, blame others (protesters, rogue police, politicians — anyone convenient) and look at the events from their point of view. If you can predict these sorts of reinterpretation, then you can plan in advance to counter them.

Lying. If police lie about what happens, you need to have good evidence to expose the lies. As a process, lying is similar to cover-up. Cover-up is hiding the truth or, in other words, lying by omission. It's a type of deception. Lying is telling a falsehood. It happens all the time. Be prepared with exactly the same sorts of preparations as for dealing with cover-up, namely ways to show people what really happened.

Police almost always believe that they must stick together. For police to inform on misbehaviour by other police is seen as the lowest act of all. Police subscribe to the police "code of silence": the rule is never to snitch on other police. That means it's okay to lie on behalf of other police.[8]

Minimising. Perpetrators of assaults often think what they've done is not nearly as serious as do the victims.[9] This could be a conscious deception — a lie — but can also be a sincere inability to see things from the point of view of those on the other side, or a sincere disagreement with their perspective. When the police use force in subduing or arresting someone, they don't think a lot about the pain and damage they cause, whereas those who

---

8   Michael W. Quinn, *Walking with the Devil: The Police Code of Silence* (Minneapolis: Quinn and Associates, 2005).
9   Roy F. Baumeister, *Evil: Inside Human Violence and Cruelty* (New York: Freeman, 1997).

are subdued or arrested are vividly aware of it, sometimes for a very long time afterwards. Police, in explaining their actions, therefore may minimise the consequences of their actions in comparison to the viewpoints of those on the receiving end.

Minimising language can be countered by being prepared to collect evidence about impacts. This includes cameras, witnesses, victim statements, photos and testimony by medical personnel. Preparation is similar to what's useful for dealing with cover-up.

Blaming. If police assaults are exposed and the negative publicity starts to hurt the police, then they may start blaming. Those involved will say someone else was responsible: police might blame their commanders or politicians; police chiefs might blame a few "rogues" or "bad apples."

How do you prepare for blaming? This depends a lot on the situation and what you want to achieve. It's easier to collect evidence about the police who use excessive force, by taking photos, collecting names and exposing individuals. However, when police are acting under orders, some responsibility lies with commanders or politicians. It's usually much harder to gather evidence about this. If you can get to know members of the police, you may be able to gain insights or even documents, such as emails, that implicate higher officials.

The more you know beforehand about who is responsible for police conduct, the more you can prepare for blaming tactics in the aftermath of police brutality. Can this make any difference beforehand? One possibility is to communicate with police, and maybe with other audiences, about responsibility for police conduct. That way, they will know that you know how to counter blaming tactics.

Framing. Police will describe what happened using their own conceptual framework. This means a set of ideas they use to make sense of the world. Police typically believe that they are doing a valuable service to the community. They may believe that unruly protest — or any protest at all — is a threat to the social order. They may believe that they must enforce the law. They may believe that protesters are the enemy, or agents of the enemy, and should be punished for their behaviour.

When police beat up protesters, they perceive this differently than protesters. Police see this as doing their job, according to commands and standard procedure. When challenged, they do not think in terms of brutality but in terms of getting their job done.

Framing is a way of thinking and often is quite sincere. Framing is not a devious technique like lying, but rather something that everyone does in one way or another.

When preparing for the possibility of police violence, you should expect there will be a clash of frames, in other words a struggle over the way to interpret what happened. It's important to be aware that the police and their supporters are seeing things entirely differently from you. If you can understand their

perspective, you may be able to come up with ways to challenge or counter it, for example by developing creative ways to frame your own perspective that appeal to audiences and either undermine or make irrelevant the police framing. Concepts like "free speech," "democracy" and "human rights" can be useful. A slogan or image may be helpful in presenting your own frame.

Protesters often believe their perspective is obvious to others. After all, they are protesting in the interests of everyone, unlike opponents. The main thing is to realise that your perspective, no matter how high-minded, is *not* obvious to others. You need to be prepared for the other side selling their own viewpoint, in many cases because they sincerely believe it. It's useful to remind yourself that nothing is obvious to everyone. Even a brutal murder does not tell a story on its own: it needs to be interpreted.

Official channels

Protesters often have an ambivalent attitude towards official channels. If official channels like grievance procedures, courts and s worked well, there would be no need to protest. For example, to stop a dangerous technology or an environmentally damaging development, all that would be required is to present a rational case to government bodies that must license the development, and the right decision would be made. However, the agencies and processes for dealing with developments are often corrupted in one way or another, either through inside influence or a pervasive ideology that serves powerful groups.

Because official channels so often don't work, people protest in order to make their views known. Protest is a non-official channel. Protest often is a repudiation of official channels.

Official channels can be pursued by protesters or by police or both. The main thing to remember is that official channels usually reduce public outrage. Sometimes you may think the benefits are worth this sacrifice. Sometimes you have no choice but to be involved, for example after being arrested. If your aim is to increase public outrage over the issue you're protesting about, then you should think in terms of mobilisation: getting more people concerned and active.

To prepare in relation to official channels, the main thing is to think through your responses to various contingencies.

- If the police use violence, do you make formal complaints? Do you take the police to court? These sorts of options are likely to reduce outrage. Far more powerful is to have a plan to publicise information about the violence to wider audiences.

- If the police use violence and this generates bad publicity for the police, then the government or the police themselves may set up an inquiry. An inquiry moves the issue of police violence from the public sphere — where members of the public discuss the issue — into a formal sphere based on rules and procedures. You can't stop an inquiry. If one is set up, you can make demands.

- The inquiry should be by an independent body — not run by the police or government.

- The inquiry should be open, with proceedings open to the media and members of the public.

If the inquiry is closed and run by the police, it will most likely be a whitewash. No one knows what is happening, so there's no publicity. Some people will want to wait to hear the findings. Meanwhile, outrage dies down.

An open inquiry gives more possibilities for maintaining attention to the issue, through media reports of hearings. Even so, you shouldn't assume this is enough, because the inquiry might support the police or give weak recommendations. You should try to use the inquiry to generate support for your cause.

To return to your original situation: you're planning a protest and need to be prepared for police violence. If the police aren't violent, the whole issue of official channels doesn't arise. If they are violent, then you need to be prepared for the possibilities concerning official channels.

Intimidation and rewards

The possibility that police will assault protesters acts as a kind of intimidation in itself, and may scare people away from joining a protest. Then there is arrest and possibly forms of individual harassment during arrest and while in jail. Afterwards, police

Protest in Sanaa, Yemen (February 3, 2011)

may select certain protesters for special attention, for example surveillance, visits and arrests.

The greatest protection against these scenarios is through preparing to document and expose abuses. Preparing for intimidation is just like preparing for police violence at a protest. For example, if, after the protest, police single out some activists for surveillance and harassment, this needs to be exposed. These activists need to behave well, because ill-tempered remarks or actions can damage credibility and be used as a pretext for police actions.

Another way to prepare for intimidation is to attract greater numbers of people to the protest. People feel safer taking action in a group. Police are usually less likely to attack a large crowd than a small group. How to attract more participants? The standard methods are getting more people to join the movement and designing an action that is attractive. If fear of police violence is a major factor, then it's worth choosing a time, place and approach that lowers the risk, for example a prominent location where lots of non-participants will be watching.

With lots of participants in a rally, there is a greater risk that some will use violence and provide a justification for police violence. Therefore, it is worth thinking of other sorts of actions, for example people wearing green clothes, singing songs, or greeting strangers in the street, that seem harmless on the surface but can symbolise solidarity.

Rewards can reduce people's incentive to do anything about injustice. Police know that if they remain loyal to their commanders — which includes adhering to the code of silence, namely not speaking about abuses by fellow officers — they are more likely to retain their jobs and obtain promotions. Some protesters become police informants; often they receive payments for their efforts.

Reprisals

Your group has taken a leading role in opposing a powerful politician. You're worried about reprisals.

This is an example of the general issue of coming under attack. This might involve surveillance, infiltration, spreading of rumours, harassment of members, confiscation of equipment, threatening messages, character assassination in the media, audits of finances, break-ins and host of other methods. They operate to make your group less effective, by damaging the group's reputation, scaring members, taking up time and effort defending, and causing dissension among members and supporters. How can you prepare in ways that ward off the attack and make the attackers wish they had never started?

Cover-up

Some attacks are made openly, as when a politician criticises your group in a television broadcast. That's easier to deal with and actually may be beneficial, giving your group more visibility.

Other attacks, though, are made in ways that hide the attackers and their methods. To counter such attacks, it is often effective to document the attacks and expose them.

- If you receive threatening messages, then obtain copies and tell people what's happening. If the messages come by email, it's easy to save them. If you receive threatening or abusive phone calls, invest in technology to make recordings of future calls of a similar type. Likewise if you receive spoken threats face-to-face: use a recorder. When you have solid evidence, you can produce a factual account — a written statement, a recording or even a video — and circulate it to anyone who would be interested, using various media. Publicising threats is worthwhile as long as your supporters are not too frightened by this information. You need to show that you're not intimidated but, instead, are prepared to stand up against the threats.

- If there is a potential for an attack through an intermediary, you should try to find out who's behind the action. For example, imagine that the police are instructed by a politician to undertake a raid against your offices. Do you have contacts among the police — or among politicians — who can give you the inside story? The more informants who are sympathetic to your cause, the harder it is for opponents to remain invisible or to disguise responsibility for their actions.

- Rumours can be a powerful means of attack, in part because no one takes responsibility for initiating them. Rumours can be about financial, sexual, ideological or other matters. For example, the rumour might be that you have links to a terrorist organisation. What can you do to expose rumour-mongering? This can be difficult and delicate. If you seem to take the rumour seriously, for example by giving a logical rebuttal, it may give it greater credibility. A different sort of response is to make fun of the rumour, for example by using images or word play that highlights the absurdity of the allegations.

- If you anticipate certain types of attacks, such as beatings or arson, think about how you can expose them. This is similar to preparing to expose police violence, except there are more possibilities.

Attack role-play

If your group has been attacked previously and you anticipate further attacks, then planning is definitely worthwhile. One thing to do is prepare for a repeat of a previous attack, so that if it occurs again, you can obtain evidence and expose it.

To prepare for other sorts of attacks, you could assign two or three members to pretend they are attackers and to imagine ways to attack your group. Then everyone breaks into teams to work out responses to each of these imagined attacks.

If attacks are a regular occurrence, it may be worthwhile running role-plays of your responses. These would be like fire drills: you do everything you would do as in an actual attack, and afterwards analyse what happened and use the experience to make better preparations.

Devaluation

Your group's reputation can be attacked in all sorts of ways. A politician could make derogatory claims and the media might run damaging stories. Claims might be made about terrorist connections, corrupt dealings, dangerous practices, sexual misdemeanours and all sorts of other things.

You can prepare for several sorts of responses.

1. Ignore the claims, because they are absurd. No one will believe them.
2. Make a rational, factual response, with documents and testimonials.
3. Counter-attack, for example by pointing out the malicious motivations of opponents.
4. Make fun of the attacks.

Cartoon by Corax used by Otpor

1. Ignore the claims

You might assume that these sorts of claims are so absurd that no one will believe them. You don't need much preparation for this response. But how will you know it's the right thing to do? It might be worth doing a small survey of your supporters and of others (neutrals) to find out about your group's reputation, and its strong and weak points. If you learn that there are some concerns already, for example about certain positions or actions taken by your group, this may indicate areas of vulnerability. These might be areas where it's more important to respond.

2. Make a rational, factual response

You can have facts on hand to counter the attack, and use them in a media release, a website, an email list and whatever other means you have for responding. To be prepared, your group needs to have people who know enough about the issues and the group to prepare a response. You need to have people with skills in writing and speaking, so you can communicate the response. It's helpful to have supporters in key places who can speak on your behalf.

For example, if you know media commentators who are sympathetic, then make sure they know enough about your group to be able to reject false claims and provide facts. If there are prominent people who support you — well-respected members of the community — make sure they are well briefed about what you say and do. Find out which ones might be willing to speak on your behalf. There might also be some people who don't support you but who believe in fair play, and who would be willing to challenge criticisms based on lies and misrepresentations. Their statements will be especially powerful because they will be seen as less self-interested.

If you are well prepared, then an attack might actually benefit your group, by mobilising all sorts of people in your defence. Just remember that they need to know enough about your group to be able to counter false claims.

3. Counter-attack

The idea here is to turn the spotlight on the attackers, showing their ulterior motives, lies, conflicts of interest, corrupt behaviour and other shortcomings. To prepare for this counter-tactic, you might prepare a "dirt file" — a collection of information damaging to your opponents — and have ways to publicise claims. For example, you might know people who have a grievance against your opponents and who are willing to speak out.

This can be a powerful approach, but you need to think carefully about whether it is the best way to proceed. One disadvantage is that you may be seen as the attacker rather than the target of attack. Instead of being purely a victim of unscrupulous politicians, audiences may simply perceive abuse being hurled from both sides, and therefore think "anything goes," namely even unsavoury tactics are acceptable.

If your opponents have more resources and are willing to use them, it may be better to avoid counter-attacking. On the other hand, if most members of the public already think your opponents are corrupt, then you don't need to worry so much — and you don't need to lead the counter-attack, because others may do it for you.

4. Make fun of the attacks

You can use humour to defuse the attacks. This could be through jokes, hoax media releases, costumes or protest stunts.

In 2000, the activist movement Otpor suffered repression from the Serbian regime led by Slobodan Milosevic. The regime said Otpor were terrorists, fascists and drug addicts. A cartoonist drew a satirical picture of Otpor as a little boy drawing a clenched fist, Otpor's symbol, on the pavement while threatened by large caricatures of Milosevic and other Serbian leaders. Otpor used the cartoon in leaflets that juxtaposed the innocent image with the regime's labels.[10]

By using humour, you send the message that these claims about your group are not to be taken seriously: they are just silly. This makes it more difficult for the attacker to continue with claims, because it may just remind people of the silliness.

The big challenge is to come up with humorous techniques that resonate with supporters and even with opponents. If the humour is seen as too nasty, it may seem like a counter-attack. Sarcasm might be misinterpreted as being serious. To be prepared to make fun of attacks, you should practise beforehand, thinking up light-hearted ways to respond. You might even come up with some ideas for actions that you can use whether there's an attack or not.

Reinterpretation

The attackers may lie about what they are doing or the reasons for it, say that what's happening is not that significant, blame others for any problems, and present their own perspective on

---

[10] Majken Jul Sorensen, "Humour as a serious strategy of nonviolent resistance to oppression," *Peace & Change*, Vol. 33, No. 2, April 2008, pp. 167–190.

what it all means. To prepare, you need to have people on your side who are familiar with the facts, clear about your group's view on the world, and who have the capacity to communicate with relevant audiences. You need to be able to back up everything your people say.

For example, if there's a raid on your offices and your computers are confiscated, the police may say it's a routine check and that nothing was taken. (They might also say the raid was about drugs, a claim that better fits into devaluation.) If you have video evidence that the police removed computers, you can expose the lie. If you have informants saying that a politician ordered the raid, you can expose another lie. You can say that the raid is an outrageous assault on democracy and free speech.

Confiscation of your computers is a serious matter, and you should be prepared. This involves planning independently of backfire analysis.[11]

Official channels

When your group comes under attack, it's likely that various laws and regulations are violated. You might be tempted to make a complaint to the police ombudsman, sue in court for defamation, make a complaint to the privacy commission, seek a ruling from parliament, or use any of a number of other formal processes. Sometimes these options are worthwhile, but they are likely to reduce outrage.

When you put in a complaint, you are relying on the system to fix the problem — to provide justice. The trouble is that the processes are usually very slow, involve a lot of time and effort and sometimes money, require the use of experts such as lawyers, and involve technicalities. You are diverted from campaigning.

If members of your group want to consider these sorts of

---

[11] For one approach, see Schweik Action Wollongong, "Safeguarding your group: a checklist," http://www.bmartin.cc/others/SAWchecklist.pdf.

options, ask them for information about the success rate of previous complaints. (Often the information isn't available.) Ask them to contact other groups that have made similar complaints, and to find out how much time, effort and money was involved. Ask them about how many people were involved in the complaint process.

Official channels sometimes are effective in their own terms, but there is an opportunity cost: there are things you didn't do because so much time and effort was tied up in the official channels. You need to think of what you could do if the same time and effort were put into campaigning. Instead of writing a submission to a government agency, imagine the same effort put into writing stories to mobilise support or organise an action.

To prepare for the raid on your office, aim to use the possibility of attack to gain greater support. Invite members to spend time in the office. Set up cameras. Back up information. Let more people know how everything operates. Introduce people to each other. Yes, preparing for a possible raid could be an opportunity to become stronger.

Intimidation

If your group comes under attack, some members may be frightened. They might be the ones attacked, or they might worry that they will be next.

To prepare, members need to be reassured. One of the best ways is to think through possible scenarios, work out responses and plan accordingly. When people know what to do, they are less afraid.

Some people are strong in a crisis. They are confident, courageous and inspiring. Some of these crisis leaders are old-timers; others are young and new to campaigning. The challenge for your group is to identify crisis leaders, prepare them for action and yet not disappoint them when nothing happens. (You don't need an internal crisis just to give a taste of action.)

Members often have good reasons to be frightened by an attack: their families and livelihood may be at risk. So think of ways they can be protected.

If intimidation is part of an attack, be sure to document everything that happens. Threats, assaults and reprisals will be seen by many outsiders as unfair. By documenting and exposing these actions, you can increase outrage. If you prepare well, carry out your plans well and have a bit of luck, the attackers may wish they had never acted.

Conclusion

The three examples — speaking out about corruption, the risk of police violence and the possibility of reprisals against your group — illustrate how to make plans to prepare for threats. You can apply the same sort of approach to all sorts of other issues, such as online censorship, sexual harassment, arrest and torture. The main thing is to think about what others will do to reduce outrage about their actions, and then think about what you can do to ensure this won't be effective.

The methods of cover-up, devaluation, reinterpretation, official channels and intimidation are general. By being involved with issues and campaigns, you will learn a lot of specific information that is essential to being effective. So don't rely on a list of rules. Think for yourself and be creative.

Being effective requires learning from experience. You can learn from what has happened to you and your group previously. It's also worthwhile talking to others and finding out what worked for them and what didn't. Which preparations made a difference? Which ones were a waste of time? And be sure to let others know the lessons from your own experience.

4. Now and afterwards

An injustice is happening right now.

- An activist has just been arrested.
- Protesters are being beaten by police.
- Illegal surveillance of citizens is being undertaken.
- False claims about activists being terrorists are being made by the government.
- People are being tortured.
- Civilians are being killed by airstrikes.

What should be done? A lot depends on the context. Activists need to know the political circumstances, the history of the issue, the situation of potential allies and likely opponents and their own capacity to mobilise action — and much else. There's no right answer to the question of what to do.

The backfire model can provide a few insights. That's all they are: ideas about what you might do. These need to be used in conjunction with your understanding of what is happening.

If you've prepared carefully for what's happening, then you just need to follow through with plans for gathering evidence, mobilising supporters, and so forth. However, some events are truly unexpected — you wouldn't think of preparing for them.

Perhaps there's publicity about a police beating or there's a media exposé about government corruption. If these are causes you care about, you may want to take action. You can predict that the perpetrators will use methods to reduce outrage. You can take action to counter these methods.

The standard five methods for increasing outrage are to expose the action, validate the target, interpret the events as an injustice, mobilise support and avoid official channels, and resist intimidation. These can be abbreviated to reveal, redeem, reframe, redirect and resist.

Reveal: expose the action

Exposing an injustice is an incredibly powerful technique. If you can reveal information, especially information that resonates with audiences, this generates popular concern that is the basis for bringing about change. Exposure sometimes is enough to stop an injustice in its tracks.

It is therefore tempting to release as much information as possible, and do it as soon as possible. However, you should always pause to think about how to be most effective. There are several factors to consider.

Consent

Suppose an activist named Helen has been arrested, without any justification — it is intimidation, pure and simple. You are prepared for a publicity campaign. But first you need to make sure Helen agrees to this campaign. If she told you beforehand, that's the consent you need — go ahead. (This is one aspect of preparing beforehand.) If you can talk to her, and she agrees — go ahead. But what if she says no? Then you should respect her request — except perhaps in exceptional circumstances. For example, you might have evidence that she is being forced to say no, or that without a campaign she is in grave danger.

A different conundrum is when you can't get in contact with Helen and you don't know what she wants. You then need to use your judgement, preferably after consultation with Helen's family and close friends.

Helen might have good reasons to say no to publicity. She

In 1930 in India, Mohandas Gandhi led a campaign against British rule by challenging the laws on salt. In one key confrontation, police severely beat nonviolent resisters. Despite British attempts to reduce outrage, reports of this action greatly weakened support for British rule.

might be afraid about derogatory information about her being released by the police, or not want her family to know, or be worried about the impact of publicity on her career. You need to respect her opinion, even if you believe publicity will be better for her. She might just feel that she doesn't want, on this occasion, to be the centre of a campaign. Not everyone does!

If you can talk with her, you can present arguments about the value of publicity. If she knows about outrage management strategies, she will be in a better position to make an informed judgement.

Quality of information

You have some preliminary reports about beatings, so you rush out a media release or inform thousands of supporters through Facebook. But what if the reports aren't correct? Then you will lose credibility, especially as a source of quality information. So it might be better to wait until the reports are confirmed.

If you are basing actions on the information, then you need to make sure the information is correct. Imagine calling thousands of supporters out on the streets on the basis of a false report.

Sometimes the information is correct, but it's not vivid. You might have reports of torture from reliable correspondents who are involved in a liberation struggle. You trust the reports because you know the correspondents. But if there are no independent witnesses, then the story might not be taken up. This situation can be changed by photographic evidence. Photos or videos of torture can be very powerful.

Should you wait until you have more vivid evidence? If you trust the evidence, then it may be worth publicising it. If you obtain more vivid evidence later, it is not a surprise but instead provides powerful reinforcement. On the other hand, if the initial evidence is unclear or confusing, then it may be better to wait for better evidence.

In late 2003, there were stories from the Red Cross and others about torture of prisoners in Afghanistan and Iraq by US prison guards. These received a little bit of mass media coverage but had little impact. Then in early 2004, dramatic photos from Abu Ghraib became available, creating one of the biggest human rights stories of the year. In amidst the commentary was the information about the early reports, revealing that the story had not received much attention until the photos were released.

Media cycles

You decide to release some dramatic information about human rights violations. However, there is hardly any mass media coverage, because that same day there was a massive earthquake. All the headlines were about the earthquake and your story was buried.

You can't predict natural disasters but you can predict some sorts of media priorities, such as elections. Major events like natural disasters may dominate coverage for days, weeks or even months.

You need to learn about the way mass media treat stories. Some days of the week and some times of the day are better for media releases. So learn about the operations of the local, national and even international media so that you can promote your information at the best possible time. Sometimes it may be better to wait until the time is right.

Social media operate in different ways and not always in the same way as the mass media. Learn about their cycles and priorities so you can get a good response.

Gradual release?

Sometimes you have lots of good material to reveal. It may be best to release it all at once, to achieve maximum impact. Another option is to release it gradually, to keep the story going longer. The impact of spreading out disclosures is shown by the way some newspapers ran stories, over days or weeks, based on WikiLeaks documents.

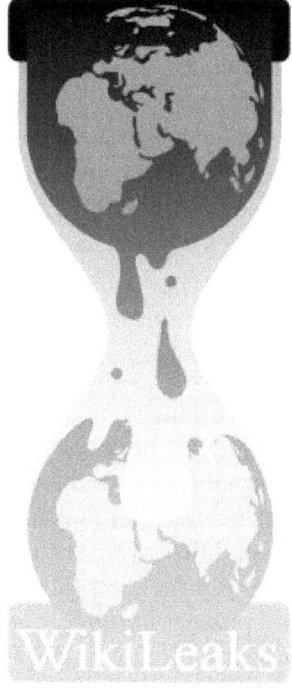

The basic point here is to think about how to be effective in disclosing information. Sometimes you have little control over this, but when you do, think about your options. Immediate exposure is highly tempting, but it can worthwhile to wait until a more opportune time, for better information or until people support your plans.

Redeem: validate the target

As the injustice proceeds, be prepared for the other side to try to discredit you, your group or whoever you're supporting. You need to be prepared to protect your reputation.

Your behaviour is crucial. If you are accused of being a crazy destroyer, it can be effective to behave calmly and dress respectably. Your sensible, polite behaviour confounds the claims and make your attackers seem to be the crazy ones.

Your language is crucial. If you are being subject to verbal abuse, it is tempting to reply the same way, using inflammatory rhetoric. This may not matter, but it's worth thinking of how your language maintains, indeed creates, your image. You may decide to speak logically and carefully, or emotionally and passionately, or with empathy and compassion. As long as you don't counter-attack, you have an advantage. Styles of speech depend a lot on cultural patterns and expectations, and there's no general rule for all situations. The key thing is that your verbal style can play an important role in countering attempts to devalue you.

Evidence of your honesty, performance or commitment can be helpful. What your supporters say is crucial. If they have evidence of your sincerity and good works, and openly vouch for you, this is powerful support against attempts to discredit.

Example

Scott Parkin, a nonviolent activist from Texas, visited Australia in 2005. Without warning, he was arrested and held pending deportation. Australian government officials made statements suggesting Parkin was involved in violent protest.

Iain Murray, an Australian nonviolent activist who was planning to meet Scott for a training session that morning, organised protests in support of Scott. He was careful to refer to Scott as a "friend" and to emphasise Scott's commitment to nonviolence. At one protest in support of Scott, protesters wore masks,

Protesters opposing the arrest and deportation of Scott Parkin

a humorous tactic that sent a message about Scott's and their own commitment to nonviolence. Iain's attention to language and behaviour helped to counter the Australian government's attempts at devaluation. Because of Iain's shrewd use of methods, along with other activists, Scott's arrest and deportation generated far more attention and support for nonviolence than would have happened otherwise. The Australian government's actions backfired.[1]

Reframe: interpret the events as an injustice

You need to explain what's happened, from your point of view. This is crucial, because opponents will lie, minimise, blame and frame things their way.

You might think the injustice is obvious. There are pictures on television. Everyone saw what happened. Surely the facts speak for themselves. Wrong! Facts never speak for themselves. They need to be interpreted. What is obvious to you may be perceived quite differently by others.

---

1   Brian Martin and Iain Murray, "The Parkin backfire," *Social Alternatives*, Vol. 24, No. 3, Third Quarter 2005, pp. 46–49, 70.

Your opponents may lie. You need to counter this by giving accurate information and exposing the lies.

Your opponents will say the issue isn't all that important. They will minimise the consequences. You need to keep saying it is important and that the consequences are serious.

If they are put on the defensive, your opponents may blame someone, usually a low-level person. Or they will blame a single leader, who becomes the scapegoat for an entire policy and widespread culpability. You need to pinpoint who is responsible.

Most importantly, your opponents will talk about the events from their own perspective, using language that encourages people to think from their point of view. You need to counter this by using your own frames. On any issue, you need to know what your goal is and whether the current topical issue is a good opportunity for promoting your perspective.

Redirect: mobilise support and avoid official channels

If outrage is great enough, the government or other powerful groups may set up an inquiry to investigate. Or they may bring out some experts to make pronouncements. Or they may tell protesters to make complaints to a police grievance procedure or to the ombudsman, or to sue in court. Or they may say to wait for an election.

What these sorts of responses have in common is an assumption that officials — in courts, inquiries, expert panels, or government agencies — will address the problem and provide justice. Most of the officials involved in these agencies are well meaning; many are highly committed to social justice. But the official channels are nearly always slow, involve all sorts of rules and regulations, and depend on the use of experts such as lawyers. They take the issue out of the public domain and put it into a special arena that is often ideally suited for sapping energy out of protest movements.

When an issue is hot, you should be aiming to promote action and to change behaviours and policies. So it's usually best not to advocate official channels. It might feel good to say "we want an inquiry into police violence" or "we want the UN to intervene" but the reality is seldom as satisfying.

Sometimes, though, the government, police or other agencies themselves set up official channels. Let's say it's a formal inquiry. What's the most effective way to respond?

Option 1: Participate in the inquiry by making submissions, testifying and encouraging others to do the same. This might help to produce better findings. The disadvantage is that energy is diverted from public campaigning. If the inquiry produces weak recommendations, having participated in the inquiry gives it greater credibility.

Option 2: Push for a better inquiry. Internal inquiries — run by agencies like the police or by the government — are most likely to serve the status quo. So demand an independent inquiry. Closed inquiries — in which the hearings are confidential, not open to the public — are the most likely to be whitewashes. So demand an open, public inquiry.

Option 3: Infiltrate the inquiry. Have supporters on the inside, such as panel members or support staff, who provide information about how the inquiry is proceeding and how best to deal with it.

Option 4: Ignore the inquiry. Continue campaigning as usual and don't be distracted.

Option 5: Try to discredit the inquiry. Point out weaknesses of the inquiry such as narrow terms of reference, misleading assumptions, conflicts of interest and inadequate powers to call witnesses and collect information.

Option 6: Carry out your own inquiry. A "people's inquiry" into police violence could have public hearings, collect evidence and make public statements.

Option 7: Use the inquiry as a campaigning opportunity. Whenever there is a significant development, hold a rally or carry out a stunt. Have members attend the inquiry to collect information or carry out an action. Arrange for a running commentary on developments, providing an alternative interpretation. With this option, your aim is to mobilise support. The inquiry is one means to help do this.

What's the best option? It depends on the situation. The most important thing is to discuss various options and consider available evidence about what will work best. What happened with previous inquiries? What do you know about the panel members? What do members of the public think?

Later, there's another time for making decisions: when the inquiry finally reports its findings.

- If the findings are not what you wanted, you need to challenge the findings — and perhaps question the fairness of the inquiry too.

- If the findings are just what you wanted, you may be faced with a greater challenge: getting the findings implemented. Many people will think, "The problem is solved because of these good recommendations" and won't feel the need to do anything. Be prepared to keep campaigning.

In a few rare cases, when everyone expects justice through an inquiry, weak findings will rekindle outrage.

After the beating of Rodney King in 1991, there was a court case against four police officers involved in the beating. Everyone expected them to be convicted. But the jury found them not guilty. The outrage over justice denied was so great that a riot erupted in South Central Los Angeles, lasting days, with over 50 people killed and hundreds of millions of dollars of property damage. Later, after a second trial of the officers, two were found guilty and there were no disturbances.

Resist intimidation

In the midst of an injustice, some people will be afraid to protest because of the risks, whether of looking foolish, losing their job, or being arrested, beaten, tortured or killed. Intimidation is a powerful tactic against protest and needs to be carefully assessed.

Several points are worth remembering.

- Consent. Anyone who resists needs to be fully aware of the risks.

- Participation. Usually it is safer to protest when more people are involved. (Greater participation, especially when a cross-section of the population is involved, also gives greater credibility to the protest — at least if everyone behaves in a way that is difficult to discredit.)

- Risk-takers. Some individuals are willing to take greater risks. In many cases, young people take the lead. It is especially important they understand the risks. They need to be supported. On the other hand, impetuous action can sometimes be counterproductive. Risk-takers are valuable to a protest movement. Their contribution should be used for maximum advantage, when really needed, and not for trivial purposes.

- Options. It is worth having different ways to protest. Some will be riskier than others. If the dangers are great, it can be good to have relatively safe ways to protest, such as turning lights on or off, banging pots and pans, or wearing clothes of a certain colour or style.

- Visibility. For some individuals, it is safer to resist openly than to keep a low profile. If you are a known dissident and at risk of arrest, then the more people who are around you, the safer you may be, because there will be witnesses if anything happens.

Intimidation can be a source of outrage. So you should try to obtain good quality, vivid evidence of intimidation and expose it to receptive audiences. If you are able to do this, you can make attacks counterproductive.

Afterwards

After the events are all over, is there anything you need to do?

The events may be over, but the struggle against injustice isn't over. The memory and meaning and impact of the events can still be disputed.

The beating of Rodney King occurred in 1991. In the following years, King was occasionally in the news, often for being arrested. In 2003, David Horowitz, a prominent commentator with right-wing views, wrote an article in which he referred to King as "a self-destructive lout," "a pathetic bum" and "a reckless criminal." Why? Because King's beating remained a symbol of police brutality. Horowitz, by denigrating King, was defending the police against critics. The beating of King was over, but its significance was still being contested.

A police beating can be remembered or forgotten. It can be seen as less of a concern if the victim — like King — is seen as a lesser person. It can be interpreted as correct procedure or abuse. It can be seen as having been dealt with appropriately or inappropriately by courts or other agencies. People can feel free to speak their views about it, or be afraid.

In 1915, during World War I, Armenians, a minority ethic group in the Ottoman Empire, were marched from their homes by Ottoman troops. A million or more died through starvation, exhaustion and massacres. This is widely seen as one of the most significant genocides of the century — but not by the

Turkish government (the Ottoman Empire's successor state), which continues to claim no genocide occurred. A century after the events, the government continues to hide information about the events and to intimidate those who interpret them as genocide. In other words, the Turkish government continues to use methods to reduce outrage over injustice.

In this sense, the Armenian genocide is not over. Its meaning, and indeed even its very occurrence, continue to be contested.

Like the beating of Rodney King and the Armenian genocide, struggles over the meaning of events can continue for years or decades. This is especially true of some events, such as the life of Jesus, European colonisation and the Holocaust, that become embedded in wider narratives about the meaning of the world.

Therefore, it is unwise to assume that because the immediate events are over, the struggle is over and it's okay to move on to other things. There is an important role for maintaining memories, validating victims, challenging reinterpretations and questioning unfair verdicts. Anniversaries of events — injustices or successful campaigns — can be occasions to rekindle concern and maintain vigilance against problems in the future. The annual rallies on 6 August, the anniversary of the dropping of an atomic bomb on Hiroshima in 1945, help maintain concern about the dangers of nuclear weapons.

Backfire analysis is one way to keep alive the memory of injustice. By exposing the techniques used to manage outrage, the memory of injustice is protected from those who prefer to hide the story, denigrate the victims and interpret the events as acceptable.

5. Questions and responses

Here are some questions relating to the backfire model, and possible answers.

The beatings were terrible. It was a gross injustice. But where was the outrage? No one cared. The model doesn't work.
The backfire model is about tactics used by perpetrators of injustice and ways to counter them. It doesn't say that people are necessarily outraged by what *you* think is an injustice.

How do you know no one cared or no one was outraged? Maybe there were complaints or protests but you didn't hear about them.

Have you examined the tactics used by the perpetrators to reduce outrage? Maybe that's the reason people didn't know about the beatings or didn't think they were so important.

Before the 2003 invasion of Iraq, there were massive protests. But the invasion went ahead anyway. The peace movement failed to stop it.
Actually, the protests made a huge difference. They showed there was massive opposition and helped discredit the invasion.

After the 9/11 terrorist attacks, worldwide support for the US government was sky-high. The invasion of Iraq squandered this good will. The protests were an important part of changing public opinion.

Originally, Bush, Cheney and others pushing for the invasion had visions of further interventions to impose their will on other countries such as Syria and Iran. The vocal opposition to the invasion of Iraq was one factor in helping scuttle this agenda.

Picture of anti-Iraq-sanctions and anti-Iraq-invasion marchers. 2002 or 2003, Washington, DC.

In preparation for the invasion, the US government used all five methods to reduce outrage. It hid evidence about Saddam Hussein's military capacity, it demonised Saddam as another Hitler and implied he was responsible for 9/11, it gave false or dubious justifications for going to war (Saddam's alleged weapons of mass destruction and al Qaeda connections), it sought endorsement from the UN (not obtained), and threatened and bribed governments on the UN Security Council to support an invasion. Without protest, these methods would have been more successful. For example, if there had been no protest, governments sitting on the Security Council might have succumbed to US government pressure, leading the Security Council to endorse an invasion, giving it much greater legitimacy and opening the door to future invasions.[1]

How about this idea? We'll plan an action that leads to activists being beaten or even killed. That will generate outrage and publicise our cause.

Planning to create a backfire is possible, but it can be risky.

---

1 Brian Martin, "Iraq attack backfire," *Economic and Political Weekly*, Vol. 39, No. 16, 17–23 April 2004, pp. 1577–1583.

Any evidence or even speculation that you are doing this can be used to discredit you. Therefore, encouraging others to attack you, in the hope of a backfire, is seldom advisable.

Instead, you can design what is called a dilemma action, in which you take action and whatever the opponent does is bad for them. The 2010 Freedom Flotilla to Gaza is an example. If the Israeli government allowed the flotilla to land in Gaza, this would break the blockade and signal the weakness of the Israeli government. But if the Israeli government stopped the flotilla, this might be seen as unjust. As it turned out, Israeli commandoes attacked, with nine passengers killed and others beaten and arrested, causing a massive backfire against the Israeli government. However, the flotilla planners didn't *hope* for an Israeli attack, nor would it be ethical to plan for deaths and serious injuries. The flotilla planner made preparations for these outcomes but there was another option for the Israeli government. A dilemma action gives the opponent a choice.

Dilemma actions need to be carefully prepared, otherwise attacks will not backfire. There was massive publicity about the flotilla. But suppose some activists go to a border expecting to be killed. If no one knows about it, or knows why they are going to the border, then killings won't backfire. Preparation is absolutely crucial.

Imagine some activists who are opposed to land mines and who decide to walk through a mined area. Some are maimed or killed. Would this backfire on the manufacturers and users of land mines? Hardly. The activists would probably be seen as misguided or stupid, because the opponents — supporters of land mines — cannot sensibly do anything.

The backfire model gives too much attention to tactics. We need to have a good long-term strategy.

True — the backfire model deals with actions taken in the short term. True — strategy is important. So let's look at the connection.

Strategy can be thought of as a plan for achieving a goal, taking into account circumstances, resources, allies and so forth. Tactics can be thought of as actions taken within the context of a strategy. So the key question is not whether there's too much focus on tactics, but rather whether the tactics used are compatible with the strategy.

The backfire model contains some implicit assumptions about strategy, most importantly that it is valuable to mobilise support via people's passions against injustice. If your strategy is compatible with this assumption, then there's no problem.

Suppose, for the sake of argument, some activists on your side are so frustrated with the lack of progress that they decide to use aggression against opponents, treating them badly or blowing them up. If this is your approach, don't use the backfire model, because the model suggests an entirely different direction.

Maybe your strategy is to do whatever you want to that makes you feel good. So if you want to dress like gorillas, shout abuse at strangers and make a mess in restaurants, go ahead — and don't use the backfire model, because it's about mobilising support, not about feeling good. (However, you should be able to work out ways to feel good while using the model.)

Strategy is vitally important. But for most activists, strategy isn't all that exciting. Doing things is. So if you care about strategy, you should think about what approaches to tactics — to action — are most compatible with an effective strategy. If the backfire approach is suitable, help others understand it. If not, then do something else.

Sometimes we do things that reduce outrage. We hide things and shout abuse. Does that mean we're perpetrators?

It's important to separate two things: (1) things that are seen as unjust, like beatings and massacres; (2) methods used to reduce outrage over things seen as unjust.

If you're beating up people or shooting them, then you're definitely a perpetrator. Others are likely to see you as the problem.

Imagine you join a protest action and police beat you very

Israeli forces violently dispersed a Hebron demonstration, firing tear gas and sound bombs and arresting one German solidarity activist

badly. You decide, for personal reasons, not to tell anyone. Perhaps you don't want your family or your employer to know you were protesting. So you've contributed to cover-up. That doesn't mean you're the perpetrator. It just means you haven't exposed the beating, and outrage is likely to be less than it would be otherwise. It's your choice.

Imagine that you join a protest and shout nasty slogans about the police. Are you a perpetrator? Yes, but only of shouting nasty slogans. This isn't nearly as serious as a brutal beating. The main issue is whether it's a good tactic to shout nasty slogans. It might make some observers think the beating was justified.

When someone challenges you and says, accusingly, "You're covering up" or "You're using official channels," you can answer, "What's the problem?" You're using methods that reduce outrage, but you might have good reasons.

When someone says, "You're using intimidation," you need to consider their claim carefully. If what you're doing is threatening to others, maybe you're doing the wrong thing. On the other hand, maybe they are powerful perpetrators and you're using nonviolent action to challenge their actions. They might disagree with your viewpoint or think that civil disobedience is a dangerous threat to the social order, and feel threatened.

Methods that reduce outrage are not automatically bad. Each case needs to be considered on its merits. So when labels are used ("cover-up," "intimidation"), be sure to look at what's really going on.

I'm in a group about to embark on a campaign that I think is misguided, based on my experience. My ideas agree with backfire model. How can I use the model to encourage members to support an approach more likely to achieve our group's aims?

You can try to initiate a discussion of options for the group. You might say, "The backfire model suggests that it would be better to avoid official channels. Maybe we should think about this more before proceeding." Discussion is often valuable.

You need to be open to different ideas. You need to listen as well as present your view. Maybe the backfire model is wrong in this case, or other considerations are more important.

However, if you've listened and discussed and argued on and on, but the others are intent on continuing, here are some possibilities.

- Ask them for evidence — from other campaigns — that their plan will work.

- Make a prediction about what will happen. Write it down. If your prediction comes true, you can say, "I told you!" (This may not make you popular, however.)

- Suggest doing a small experiment trying different methods, before starting on the major campaign.

- Ask them what evidence would change their minds. If they can't think of any, you know that motivations or deep beliefs are more important than evidence.

After all this, you may find they are simply not listening. Maybe they think you are a pain in the neck for continuing to question the campaign they are committed to. Then what?

Option 1. Join in the campaign. Do what you can to help make it successful. Sometimes it's more important to work together as a group, and fail, than to be effective in the short term but then for the group to break up due to internal disagreements and disputes. In the long term, working together may be the best option. Maybe everyone will learn from failures. (Maybe not!)

Option 2. Sabotage their efforts, because they are seriously misguided. This is a very bad option. To even think about it suggests you've lost perspective and need to move on —

Option 3. Leave the group and join another, or set up your own group. Or just work alone. No more disagreements!

6. Exercises

You can work on these exercises individually or in a group. In a workshop, several people or groups can work simultaneously on an exercise, comparing responses.

1. Analyse an injustice

Select an injustice that you, or someone in your group, know a lot about. It could be from personal experience, like bullying at school, from study, such as the Holocaust, or from campaigning on an issue, such as child soldiers.

(a) Write down methods used by the perpetrators that reduce outrage, under the five categories of

- cover-up
- devaluation
- reinterpretation
- official channels
- intimidation.

(b) Write down methods actually used by the targets to increase outrage, under the five categories of

- reveal (expose the action)
- redeem (validate the target)
- reframe (interpret the events as an injustice)
- redirect (mobilise support and avoid official channels)
- resist (resist intimidation)

(c) Write down the source of your information/knowledge about each of these methods, for example observation, conversations, news broadcasts, lectures or history books.

(d) Write down how you could find out more about the methods used.

(e) Write down methods that *could* be used by targets to increase outrage (even if they weren't used at the time).

(f) Think about or discuss whether classifying the methods helps in understanding what happened concerning the injustice.

2. Study a backfire article

Pick an article that uses backfire analysis.[1]

(a) Write a short summary of the key ideas in the article. This might be a list of methods of reducing and increasing outrage.

(b) Assess the analysis. How is evidence used? Are methods classified sensibly? Is the conclusion well supported? What would you change to make the article more rigorous, informative or persuasive?

(c) Examine the article's style. Is it academic or popular? Is it clearly expressed? Does it use a narrative (story) or some other way of presenting information? What would you change to make the article more suitable for a specific audience, for example school children or military veterans?

(d) Read another article on the same issue, one that doesn't

---

[1] For many possibilities, see "Backfire materials," http://www.bmartin.cc/pubs/backfire.html

use backfire analysis, for example from a news report. Is there any new information that could be incorporated into the backfire-analysis article? Is there any information that challenges the backfire analysis? Does the new article reveal any methods that don't easily fit the backfire model?

3. Make a comment

Choose an opportunity to comment on an article or news story dealing with injustice, for example a blog or online article. Post a comment using ideas from the backfire model. For example, you might comment on how an action backfired, how devaluation is being used, or what framing has been adopted. (You don't need to mention the backfire model at all. Just point to tactics or consequences.) Look at subsequent comments to see whether anyone responds to what you've said. Seek to make comments that stimulate thoughtful responses and a more informed discussion.

4. Write a backfire analysis

The following steps are suggestions. Modify them to suit your needs.

(a) Choose a topic you already know something about, or read one or two basic articles.

(b) Choose a format, for example article, slide show or poster.

(c) Write a first draft drawing entirely on your knowledge, without consulting any sources.

(d) Read or check several additional sources, modifying your draft as you proceed, revising and editing along the way.

(e) When the draft is reasonably coherent and polished, give or present it to one or two non-experts, seeking their questions and comments. Make revisions.

(f) Give or present the draft to some people knowledgeable about the topic. Make revisions based on their comments.

(g) If both non-experts and experts think what you've done is satisfactory, you can use or present your analysis. If not, cycle through steps d to f again.

Tip: start small, so you can finish in a reasonable time. When you gain more experience, you can tackle a larger project.

5. Plan for an attack

(a) Imagine a possible attack, for example something damaging done to you personally, to your group, or to some person or group you care about.

(b) Write down the things the attacker could do to reduce outrage about the attack.

(c) Write down how you, your group or someone else could increase outrage.

(d) Write down the most important ways to prepare for the attack.

(e) Decide when, where and how these preparations are going to happen.

(f) If the preparation is something you can do personally, then do it! If others need to take action, work out a plan to encourage them to do it.

6. Play a game of tactics

It helps to have two or more people for this exercise.

(a) Break into two teams, an attack team and a defence team. Decide on a general type of attack.

(b) The attack team — naturally! — thinks up a creative ways to attack, including ways to reduce outrage. The defence team imagines ways to prepare that would counter the attack and increase outrage.

(c) The teams compare their ideas.

Depending on the scenario, the defence team could wait to hear the attack team's plans, or both teams could prepare simultaneously.

7. Make predictions

Watch the media, and pick out a prominent breaking story that involves potential wrongdoing by a powerful group. Examples from 2011 included assaults on Egyptian protesters, the hacking scandal involving News Corporation and the charges against WikiLeaks founder Julian Assange.

(a) As the story breaks, make predictions about the sorts of methods used by the powerful group that reduce outrage.

(b) Seek more information, from various sources, or wait for further revelations, and see whether your predictions are correct.

8. Have a conversation

Sometimes you meet someone who is heavily involved in opposing an injustice. They might work in a rape crisis centre, campaign on environmental issues or be an active member of Amnesty International. If you have a chance to talk with them for a while, ask them about their issue, using backfire categories. Here are some possible questions, with "they" referring to opponents, such as rapists, polluting companies or repressive governments.

- Do they cover up information about their activities?
- Do they try to devalue the targets?
- Do they lie about what they've done? Do they minimise its significance? Do they blame others? Do they see things from a completely different viewpoint?
- How well do formal processes like government agencies and courts work to fix the problem?
- Do they use threats and attacks to intimidate people?

9. Make up your own exercise!

Appendix: Human shields and pre-emptive backfire
Jørgen Johansen

When humans use their physical presence to protect possible targets, such as buildings, they are called "human shields." The idea is that if "innocent" or "well respected" citizens stay close to a possible target, the opponent will be hesitant to attack because of the possibility of a backfire effect.

Human targets

Civilians who protect other civilians are often referred to as "unarmed bodyguards". Organisations like Nonviolent Peaceforce and Peace Brigades International sponsor and support volunteers to serve as human shields for activists who are under threat by the state, guerrilla groups, mafias or paramilitaries. Such organisations have a great record of effective work.[1] On the few occasions when unarmed bodyguards are attacked, their group's well documented and respected history makes it difficult to devalue or intimidate them.

One of the main activities of these groups is to document what they are doing so it is difficult for attackers to cover up any harm done. Such organisations have a well-developed system to distribute information about their activities. Since well-respected people are either directly involved or function as ambassadors for the work, it is also difficult to reinterpret what has been done by lying, blaming and framing.

---

1   Liam Mahony and Luis Enrique Eguren, *Unarmed Bodyguards: International Accompaniment for the Protection of Human Rights* (West Hartford, CT: Kumarian Press, 1997).

Buildings and infrastructure

In war situations, humans are sometimes used as shields to protect buildings and infrastructure.

When NATO started to bomb Serbia on 24 March 1999, hundreds of local and international activists soon came to stand on the bridges in Belgrade, Grdelica, Novi Sad and other cities

The Human Shield Action to Iraq crossed the border into northern Iraq from Syria on the 15th of February, 2003. This is a picture of the crowd that greeted the double-decker buses as they made their way over the border crossing into the adjacent street. It was quite a crowd considering no one knew, not even the shields themselves until the night before, that this was where they would enter Iraq. The man leaning out the door is 68 year old Godfrey Meynell of Britain, who was fluent in Arabic and explained to the forming crowd why they were there.

in an attempt to prevent them from being destroyed by bombs. Some of the foreigners came from countries whose militaries took part in the bombing. Since several international media were present, NATO commanders avoided targeting bridges with people on them. Many other parts of the infrastructure were destroyed, but these bridges were saved.

In January 2003, prior to the impending invasion of Iraq, 30 human shield volunteers left London for Iraq to stay in Baghdad in anticipation of the bombing. During their bus journey through Europe they picked up many more activists and had a peak of approximately 500 who wanted to protect bombing targets in Iraq. They decided to stay at two water plants, two power plants, a food silo, a communication facility and an oil refinery.[2] Their goal was to prevent attacks by making it well known that they would be living at, in or close to these installations. Of these sites, only one was bombed in 2003: the communications facility, a day after the human shields left.

Nature

Some struggles against deforestation have used the technique of human shields to protect trees. In India, women from the Chipko movement in Garhwal Himalayas started in the early 1970s to "hug trees" when loggers came to cut them down. The earliest example of this kind of action can be traced back to 1731 when Amrita Devi led hundreds of people to protect threatened trees in their community.

Modern environmental activists have developed this further. Some of them live up in trees for weeks in order to make it difficult for forest companies to cut them down. Others have buried their bodies, except their heads, in deep holes in the forest road to discourage timber transports from taking the timber out. For the large trucks to pass, they must drive over and kill the activists. Some of these campaigns have been successful; others are still going on.

Conclusion

These three types of human shields use the backfire effect in a pre-emptive way. They deliberately put themselves at great risk and hope that adverse publicity from harming or killing them will be too high for the people in power. Though this sort of technique is not guaranteed to work, careful preparation can improve the likelihood of success. Campaigners plan their ac-

2 http://www.humanshields.org

tions so those in power will face great difficulties when they try to prevent popular outrage.

1. Through well-prepared documentation and effective dissemination, campaigners make it difficult for the opponent to cover up atrocities.
2. They try to engage well-respected people to reduce devaluation of the group carrying out the actions.
3. With good access to mainstream media and as well as alternative media channels, they limit the options for their opponents to lie, blame, and reframe the actions.
4. Whenever possible, they build relations with official bodies like embassies, international organisations and governments.

Some devaluation campaigns against such actions focus on the lack of volunteer participation. For example, the attackers sometimes proclaim that the human shields have been ordered to take part. Often the devaluation has taken the form of rumours that the participants will be punished if they refuse and rewarded if they take part. Others are called naive or accused of collaborating with the "enemy." The more transparency and the more well-respected people who take part, the less effect such accusations have. More experimentation and research are needed to improve the use of human shields.

www.ingramcontent.com/pod-product-compliance
Ingram Content Group UK Ltd.
Pitfield, Milton Keynes, MK11 3LW, UK
UKHW022212230426
12048UKWH00016BA/802